PETER PUCK'S
BIG BOOK OF
HOCKEY

Also by Brian McFarlane

PETER PUCK'S
BIG BOOK OF
HOCKEY
FASCINATING FACTS
FOR HOCKEY FANS OF ALL AGES

by PETER PUCK
WITH BRIAN McFARLANE

Fenn Publishing Company Ltd.
TORONTO, CANADA

Fenn Publishing Company Ltd.

A Fenn Publishing Book / First Published in 2010
Copyright 2010 © Brian McFarlane

TM & © 2010 Hanna-Barbera.
All Rights Reserved.
Licensed by Sports Family Ltd.

Fenn Publishing Company Ltd.
Bolton, Ontario, Canada
www.hbfenn.com

The publisher gratefully acknowledges the support of the Canada Council for the Arts and the Ontario Arts Council for its publishing program. We acknowledge the support of the Government of Ontario through the Ontario Media Development Corporation's Ontario Book Initiative.

ONTARIO ARTS COUNCIL
CONSEIL DES ARTS DE L'ONTARIO

The Canada Council   Le Conseil des Arts
for the Arts   du Canada
SINCE 1957   DEPUIS 1957

We acknowledge the financial support of the Government of Canada through the Canada Book Fund (formerly Book Publishing Industry Development Program) for our publishing activities. Care has been taken to trace ownership of copyright material in this book and to secure permissions. The publishers will gladly receive any information that will enable them to rectify errors or omissions.

Text design: Alison Carr

Library and Archives Canada Cataloguing in Publication

McFarlane, Brian, 1931-
          Peter Puck's big book of hockey : fascinating facts for hockey fans of all ages / Brian McFarlane.

ISBN 978-1-55168-351-5

          1. Hockey--Miscellanea. 2. National Hockey League--Miscellanea. 3. Peter Puck (Fictitious character). I. Title.

GV847.M437 2010   796.962   C2010-905086-X

Printed and bound in Canada
10 11 12 13 14 5 4 3 2 1

To all the boys and girls—and old timers, too—
who love the game as I do. Play fair and have fun!

Contents

Introduction

Men and women have been bouncing me around hockey rinks for over a hundred years and I never get bent out of shape about it. And I never get tired of being in the thick of the action.

I'm one inch thick and three inches in circumference, I weigh about six ounces, and I'm virtually indestructible. You all know me, don't you? I'm the imp of the ice, the poke check professor—I'm Peter Puck, and I'm what hockey's all about.

I love the fact that you can't have a hockey game without a Peter Puck.

I've seen some amazing events in hockey in my time, and I'm here to tell you about many of them. There was the team that travelled more than 6,450 kilometres (4,000 miles) to play for the Stanley Cup, only to lose by the highest score imaginable. There was Canada's 1924 team at the Olympics—a team that outscored the opposition 110–3 in just five games. The star player on that team averaged seven goals per game. Another Canadian team walloped poor Denmark at the World Championships by a score of 47–0.

I was on the ice at Lake Placid in 1980 when a bunch of American college kids stunned the Russians and created a "Miracle on Ice."

At the Vancouver 2010 Olympics, I was on the blade of

Sidney Crosby's stick when he zapped me past U.S. goalie Ryan Miller in overtime to bring Canada a gold medal.

There isn't much I haven't seen in hockey: Gordie Howe playing in the NHL when he was a grandfather, Henri Richard winning 11 Stanley Cups, Wayne Gretzky skating off with 61 records, Darryl Sittler scoring 10 points in a game, Bill Mosienko scoring three goals in 21 seconds, and defenceman Bobby Orr leading the NHL in scoring, not once but twice.

And there were the bizarre moments. The goalie who wore boxing gloves. The puck—one of my distant relatives—that fell through a hole in the ice and could not be found. The official who wanted to have all pucks painted green. The baseball umpire who won a Stanley Cup. The forward who scored only 53 career points and was still inducted into the Hockey Hall of Fame.

Hockey has such a rich and fascinating history, the stories keep on coming.

There are lots of interesting facts and anecdotes from my personal experience in the pages ahead. I know you are going to enjoy them. I'm hoping my friend Don Cherry will give me "two thumbs up" as an author.

And remember what Peter Puck says: Love that hockey game!

Love That Hockey History! ONE

Let's begin with some little-known facts about the history of the game. You may not have liked history class in school, but I bet you'll love my stories and facts about old-time hockey. Some of these facts are really hard to believe. But take it from me, Peter Puck, the old puck professor, they're all true.

● **How about this account** of a hockey game played in Kingston, Ontario, back in 1856? The Kaitling Pasture Wildcats and the Belle Island Barbarians met on the river ice with bent sticks and a rubber ball. Red McDuffy and Hornet Hank McIntosh collided before the opening face-off and McDuffy smashed McIntosh with his stick. McIntosh returned the compliment by kicking McDuffy in the shins with his skates and McDuffy howled in pain. A reporter wrote: "He then smote McIntosh mightily across the nether regions." The pair started a wild fight that was quelled only when McDuffy fell through a hole in the ice and almost drowned. He was rescued and carried away and the game commenced—and went on for several hours.

The reporter at the scene claimed the referee swallowed his whistle, which is a surprise because most referees used handbells in that era. (Perhaps he really swallowed *that*.)

No winner was declared because neither team could count to more than 10.

● **On March 3, 1875,** in Montreal, a group of McGill students, led by a man named James Creighton, played the first ever game of organized hockey. The game took place indoors at the stately Victoria Skating Rink, the sides were limited to nine players per team, and a number of rules were adopted. In outdoor shinny at the time, any number could play. For the indoor game, the rubber ball customarily used to score goals was replaced by a flat, circular piece of wood—a puck.

Goals were devised—two poles or flags planted in the ice—and it's possible that hockey's first two goaltenders appeared in this game.

Later came uniforms, team positions, more rules and referees.

Others may argue the point, but Creighton, who organized the game, deserves the title "Father of Canadian Hockey."

● **Here's another account** of a game played in Quebec City in 1895. Ottawa edged Quebec 3–2 and the crowd became very hostile toward the referee, a man named Hamilton. After the game, a number of fans chased after Hamilton and captured him just as he was about to board a train for Montreal. They dragged him back to the arena and tried to force him to declare the match a draw. Fortunately, police rescued the frightened official. They escorted him back to the train station and he happily fled the city.

● **In 1902,** the Toronto Wellingtons travelled to Winnipeg, where they met the Victorias in a best-of-three series for hockey's most famous trophy—the Stanley Cup. The Wellingtons lost the series, but one of their players scored a most unusual goal. When the puck split in two (they weren't as sturdy as we are today), Toronto's Chummy Hill fired half the puck into the Winnipeg net. The referee hesitated, and then signalled a goal. Imagine scoring a Stanley Cup goal with half a puck! I'm glad that puck wasn't me. The score was 5–3 for Winnipeg, but I always figured it should have been 5–2 ½.

● **Can you believe it?** Some players sitting on the bench in that Toronto–Winnipeg series were said to be puffing on cigarettes. Smoking! Smoking wasn't a no-no back then— not like it is today.

● **When the puck flew** over the low boards into the crowd, a man kept it. Yep. Put it in his pocket as a souvenir. The fans booed him and called him a poor sport for not throwing it back on the ice. Now everybody keeps the pucks that fly into the crowd. I've lost a lot of relatives that way.

● **Two months later,** in a follow-up series, the Winnipeg champs lost the Cup on home ice to a team from Montreal. More than 500 fans back in Montreal, anxious to hear the scores, filled a hall where they followed the telegrapher's reports from Winnipeg. No radio, television, or Internet in those days, folks. And hundreds more huddled outside the hall, eagerly awaiting the outcome.

● **In many** of the Stanley Cup matches in the early 1900s, spring weather made for atrocious ice conditions. Sometimes there'd be mud showing and pools of water on the indoor rink, which was quite common. In one playoff game, the puck fell through a hole in the ice and could not be recovered. There went another of my distant cousins. In Toronto one spring, in a game played indoors, there was so little ice covering the floor that players were said to be "running back and forth on the board floor."

● **After another** playoff game played in watery conditions, a reporter wrote, "Thanks to the good work of the life savers, all the players were saved from drowning." My great grandfather, Percy Puck, played in that game. He wore swimming trunks and earplugs. Just kidding, guys!

● **Montrealers have always** had a passion for hockey and have always been rabid supporters of their hometown teams. No doubt their enthusiasm is responsible, at least in part, for the record number of Stanley Cups—24—that have found their way to Montreal.

Shortly after the turn of the 20th century, there was so much excitement in Montreal over a playoff game with Ottawa that 4,000 fans outside the arena couldn't wait for the doors to open. So they made a mad rush on the building, smashed down the doors, broke the windows, and streamed into the arena without buying tickets for the big game. It was impossible for ushers and other officials to throw them out, so the game was played before a full house, even though many of the spectators were freeloaders.

● **In one early** Stanley Cup playoff game, a team from Rat Portage (now Kenora, Ontario) travelled east to play for the Stanley Cup against the powerful Ottawa team. The canny coach of the visitors decided to put two goalies in the net—at the same time. When officials said he couldn't do that, he replied, "Yes, I can. I've checked the rule book. I'll simply replace one of my forwards with a second goalie." When the two goalies stood side by side, they looked formidable. Then the game began. After a few rushes on goal, the Ottawa boys discovered they had nothing to fear. The two goalies stumbled into each other and knocked each other off balance when blocking shots. Ottawa won easily and the two-goalie experiment was quickly abandoned.

● **In a game** between Rat Portage (Kenora, Ontario) and Ottawa in 1905, the referee donned a hard hat to protect himself from objects thrown from the stands. During the same game, Rat Portage accused Ottawa officials of "salt-ing the ice" to slow down the visiting team.

● **A hundred years ago,** ice buildup on rinks would often become a problem. In 1909, the ice at an Edmonton rink was 18 inches thick, so the arena owners hired a Calgary man who'd invented an ice-shaving machine. He used his amazing machine to remove several inches of surface ice, creating ideal conditions for a forthcoming playoff game.

● **You may be surprised** to learn that the first artificial ice rink, the Glaciarium, was constructed in the Chelsea neighbourhood of London, England, in 1876. The first one in North America was at Madison Square Garden in New York in 1879.

● **Skates have** an incredibly long history. The oldest pair of skates discovered—made from the leg bones of large animals, with holes in the bones for leather straps to slide through—date back to roughly 3000 BC. Historians say the bone skates were retrieved from the bottom of a lake in Switzerland. Probably thrown there by a Swiss chap who found them too slippery to skate on.

● **The following** rule changes were proposed at the turn of the century by the president of the Ottawa club, Mr. T. Emmett Quinn.

1. To increase scoring opportunities, the puck should be painted green and reduced to half its present size, thus making it more difficult for goaltenders to see and to stop.
2. Players should be compelled to carry enough bills in their pockets to pay any fines they may receive on the spot.
3. Instead of giving a player a minor penalty, the referee should stop the play, take the offender to the side-boards and have an earnest discussion with him for a half a minute, so that he might reform him.

Mr. Quinn thought the proposed changes were good ones, but his colleagues disagreed and voted them down unanimously.

Hmm. Peter Puck painted green? Hockey pants with pockets? And Peter Puck crunched to half his present size? Yikes! No thank you, Mr. Quinn.

● **Was it murder** on ice? In a 1907 game between Ottawa and Cornwall in Cornwall, Ontario, the home team's star

player, Owen McCourt, was struck over the head with a
stick. He collapsed, and died a few hours later. Ottawa's
Charlie Masson was charged with manslaughter but was
later acquitted when witnesses failed to confirm it was his
stick that ended McCourt's life.

It shows what can happen when players swing their
sticks recklessly. You've gotta play fair, I always say. And
players should show respect for their opponents. Hockey is
played for fun. It's not a life-and-death affair.

● **What a season** for Ernie Russell! In 1906–07, the
Montreal Wanderers sniper scored 42 goals in nine games,
or more than four per game, as the Wanderers won all 10
games they played, averaged over 10 goals per game, and
won the Stanley Cup over the Kenora (formerly Rat Portage,
Ontario) Thistles. Imagine a team scoring more than 100
goals in a 10-game season.

● **During the 1910–11** season, Renfrew Creamery Kings owner M. J. O'Brien, a multi-millionaire, offered a team bonus of $100 for each goal scored in an important game against Ottawa and a personal reward of $50 to every player who scored one. Spurred by the owner's promise, Renfrew walloped Ottawa 17–2 and O'Brien cheerfully doled out $2,250 in bonus money, a fortune in that era. It was in this game that Renfrew star Fred "Cyclone" Taylor was said to have scored a goal while skating backwards.

● **In those early years,** the goal judge stood on the ice behind the goal. And when the puck went in, he waved a handkerchief in the air to signal a score. Sometimes, players rushing in behind the net would bowl him over and send him skidding along the ice.

● **In 1911,** at a meeting of the National Hockey Association, the league that preceded the NHL, it was agreed that three periods of 20 minutes would be played instead of two 30 minute periods which had been the custom.

● **Many years ago,** two small towns in Ontario developed a fierce hockey rivalry. Whenever Brantford played Preston, winning was so important that on at least one occasion an attempt was made by the fans to bribe the referee. Midway through one bitterly fought game, referee Jimmy Fraser was offered $10 if he'd "make sure Brantford wins." When he declined the money and Preston squeezed out a one-goal victory, Fraser was approached again. This time he was offered $15 if he'd report to the OHA that the winning goal was scored after time had expired. Once again, Fraser declined the bribe.

Hurrah for referee Fraser. Honesty is always the best policy.

● **In 1911,** brothers Lester and Frank Patrick boldly formed the professional Pacific Coast Hockey Association with teams in Vancouver, Victoria, and New Westminster. New indoor arenas sprang up in Vancouver and Victoria. Both rinks held artificial ice—the first in Canada.

● **When the PCHA** was introduced in 1911, fewer than 30 players were required to fill all three rosters. Most players played for 60 minutes back then. And when they weren't playing, they often acted as referees and goal judges.

● **Jack Ulrich,** who played with Victoria during the days of the PCHA, never argued with referees and never "mouthed off" at opposing players. Ulrich was deaf as a goal post.

● **Hockey was** the first team sport to introduce numbered jerseys. In 1911, the Patrick brothers, Lester and Frank, adopted the idea for their PCHA teams after watching a track meet in which the competitors wore numbers on their jerseys. Within three years, numbered jerseys were common on all teams in all leagues.

If pucks had numbers, guess who'd be number 1. That's right, me—Peter Puck.

● **In 1913,** a new rule was introduced in the National Hockey Association. Coaches were no longer allowed to use a megaphone to shout instructions to their players from the bench.

● **In 1915,** the Vancouver Millionaires became the first PCHA team to win the Stanley Cup. Playing on home ice, the Millionaires swept the eastern champion Ottawa Senators aside in three straight games and by decisive scores: 6–2, 8–3, and 12–3.

● **In 1931,** during the Great Depression, Maple Leaf Gardens opened with Chicago defeating the Leafs 2–1 in the home opener. The Gardens was called "a miracle of engineering" because it went up in six months at a cost of $1.5 million.

● **Hall of Famer** Reg Noble's hockey career began in 1916–17 and ended in 1933–34. It's his famous stick I want to tell you about. When he was traded to the Montreal Maroons, he had already used his stick for two seasons in Toronto. It must have been made of ironwood. Noble used it in another 100 games in Montreal and then was traded to Detroit where he used it for another season. Then he autographed it and presented it to the manager of the Detroit Olympia. who nailed it to the wall of his office. Later, Noble came out of retirement to play with Detroit. He broke into the manager's office, retrieved his favourite stick off the wall and used it for yet another season.

● **The longest game** in NHL history was played in Montreal on March 24–25, 1936. A playoff game between the Montreal Maroons and the Detroit Red Wings required 116 minutes and 30 seconds of overtime (six extra periods) before Detroit won 1–0. The game ended at 2:25 a.m. on a goal by Modere "Mud" Bruneteau, a two-goal scorer during the regular season.

● **On December 1, 1940,** a game in Chicago between the Black Hawks and the Rangers featured four sets of brothers. Mac and Neil Colville and Muzz and Lynn Patrick played for the Rangers. Bill and Bob Carse and Max and Doug Bentley were in uniform for the Black Hawks.

● **During the 1944–45** season, Montreal's Maurice "Rocket" Richard set a record with 50 goals in a 50-game season. On December 28, he scored five goals and three assists for a record eight points in a 9–1 romp over Detroit.

● **On November 2, 1949**, a wild fight broke out involving three Montreal Canadiens—Leo Gravelle, Billy Reay and Ken Reardon—and some angry Chicago fans at the Chicago Stadium. One fan even chased Reardon across the ice. Chicago police arrested the three Habs and tossed them in jail for an hour. They were released when they posted $200 bonds.

● **In 1950,** the New York Rangers hired Dr. David Tracy, a hypnotist, to instill confidence in the slumping Rangers. The first night he worked with the players, the Rangers lost to Boston 4–3, extending their winless streak to 13 games. Dr. Tracy was never invited back.

● **In March 1951,** Rocket Richard was fined $500 after he grabbed referee Hugh McLean by the neck in a New York hotel lobby. Richard was incensed over a penalty McLean had given him in a previous game. No punches were thrown, but there was considerable profanity.

● **In 1952–53,** Detroit's Gordie Howe took aim at Rocket Richard's 50-goal record but fell short, finishing with 49.

Right winger George Armstrong was playing so well for Toronto in 1953–54 that team owner and president Conn Smythe decided he should wear number 10, the number made famous by former Leaf captain Syl Apps. Smythe had once vowed that no other Leaf would wear the numeral.

During the 1953–54 season, Montreal's Bernie "Boom Boom" Geoffrion was suspended for 8 games (all against the New York Rangers) following a stick-swinging duel with Ron Murphy of the Rangers. Murphy, who suffered a broken jaw in the battle, received a five-game suspension.

In 1957–58, a big blond kid named Bobby Hull was the talk of Chicago. Not since teenager Gordie Howe entered the league in 1946 had a youngster looked so talented at such an early age. Hull was only 18.

In November 1961, Conn Smythe stepped aside and was succeeded as Leaf president by his son Stafford. The younger Smythe, along with partners John Bassett and Harold Ballard, handed over a $2-million cheque to Conn Smythe. Ballard took over as chairman of the Leafs' hockey committee.

On October 1963, Gordie Howe tied Rocket Richard's career goal-scoring record of 544 when he beat Habs goalie Gump Worsley at the Detroit Olympia. On November 10, he potted number 545 to become the all-time scoring champ.

In February 1965, Carl Voss, who served for 15 years as the supervisor of NHL officials, announced his retirement. He was succeeded by a popular former ref, Ian "Scotty" Morrison.

● **Chicago's Bobby Hull,** now known as "The Golden Jet," made news in 1965–66 by scoring a record 54 goals during the season.

● **In 1966,** the Boston Bruins opened the coffers to sign Bobby Orr, the best junior defenceman in Canada. Alan Eagleson, Orr's agent, negotiated a deal for a reported $25,000 at a time when the average NHL rookie salary was $8,000.

● **In 1967–68** the NHL doubled in size. The six new teams—Pittsburgh Penguins, St. Louis Blues, Philadelphia Flyers, California Seals, Los Angeles Kings and the Minnesota North Stars formed the NHL's West Division. The original six teams played in the East Division. Most experts agreed that the new owners paid a heavy price to join the league: the expansion fee was US$2 million.

● **During the first season** of expansion, in 1967–68, youthful Scotty Bowman took over as coach of the St. Louis Blues, marking the beginning of the most successful coaching career in NHL history.

● **On November 7, 1968** the Blues' Red Berenson became the second NHL player to score six goals in a game and the first to do it in a road game. He scored six against Philadelphia in an 8–0 shutout. In 1944, Syd Howe of Detroit scored six goals in a game to set the modern-day record.

● **During a** preseason game in September 1969, Boston Bruins defenceman Ted Green was involved in a bloody stick fight with St. Louis Blues forward Wayne Maki. Green was struck in the head, suffering a fractured skull and brain damage, and missed the remainder of the season, during which Boston won the Stanley Cup. Though Green was not officially eligible, his teammates gave him his share of the prize money and his name was engraved on the Cup in 1970.

● **During the 1970–71** season, Roy Spencer, father of Leafs rookie Brian Spencer, was killed in a shootout with RCMP officers outside a TV station in British Columbia. He opened fire after protesting the TV station's decision to broadcast a Vancouver–California game rather than the Toronto–Chicago game in which his son Brian was playing.

● **In 1971–72,** Scotty Bowman took over as Montreal coach, replacing Al MacNeil, whose reward for winning the Stanley Cup the previous season was a job behind the bench of the Nova Scotia Voyageurs in the American league. The Cup champs were not happy with MacNeil's coaching.

● **In 1972,** two great Bobbys—Hull and Orr—were unable to play for Team Canada in what turned out to be an electrifying series of eight games with the Soviet Union's best players. Hull was ruled ineligible because he had jumped to the WHA, and Orr was recuperating from a knee operation. Team Canada made a miraculous comeback to win the series with a last-minute goal by Paul Henderson.

● **During the 1972–73** season, NBC TV carried the NHL *Game of the Week* with Ted Lindsay, Tim Ryan, and Brian McFarlane in the broadcast booth.

It wasn't long before NBC introduced the real star of those telecasts—Peter Puck. I got tons of fan mail. One viewer wrote, "Dear Peter: Does it hurt when they hit you on your bottom?" Another wanted to know if I was married.

● **When Bobby Orr** retired in November 1978 after a brilliant 12-year career with Boston and Chicago, he had won the Norris Trophy eight times as the NHL's top defenceman, the Hart Trophy three times as league MVP, and the Art Ross Trophy twice as the individual scoring champ. And he did it after surgeons performed six operations on his wonky knees. The Hockey Hall of Fame waived the mandatory three-year waiting period for induction and Orr was enshrined at age 31, one of only 10 players to get in without having to wait three years.

Bobby, you were the best!

● **In the 1979–80 season,** Toronto manager Punch Imlach traded Lanny McDonald, one of the most popular Leafs ever, to the Colorado Rockies. Leaf players tore up their dressing room when they heard the news, and team leader Darryl Sittler was so upset at losing his friend and linemate that he immediately resigned as captain.

● **The "Miracle on Ice"** was a name given to a stunning hockey upset at the 1980 Olympics, held at Lake Placid, New York, on February 22. The American team, made up of college players and led by coach Herb Brooks, defeated the Soviet powerhouse, which was considered the best hockey team in the world. In the four Olympics after the Soviet squad had been upset by Team USA at Squaw Valley in 1960, Soviet teams had won 22 games, lost 2 and outscored the opposition 175–44. Team USA went on to win the gold medal by winning their final match over Finland. As part of its 100th anniversary celebrations in 2008, the International Ice Hockey Federation chose the Miracle on Ice as the number one international hockey story of the century.

● **On November 28, 1982,** rookie Ron Sutter made NHL history when he played in his first game for the Philadelphia Flyers. It marked the first time that five brothers served teams in the NHL.

● **Wayne Gretzky** made headlines on November 22, 1986, when he reached 500 career goals in just 575 games. Mike Bossy of the Islanders had set the previous mark— 500 goals in 647 games.

● **During the 1986–87** season, owner Harold Ballard of the Maple Leafs banned reporters from the team's dressing room following home games at Maple Leaf Gardens. Scott Morrison of the *Toronto Sun* noted, "There are 119 pro sports teams in North America and 118 allow reporters in their dressing rooms." Ballard cursed all reporters who disagreed with his edict.

● **International hockey** suffered a black eye early in 1987 when Canada and Russia became involved in a bench-clearing brawl at the World Junior Championships in Czechoslovakia. Incredibly, officials turned out the arena lights while the referee and linesmen fled to their dressing room, leaving others to deal with the problem.

● **Not long after** the Edmonton Oilers won the Stanley Cup in 1988, Wayne Gretzky learned from his father that the Oilers were planning to deal him to another team. Walter Gretzky had known for some time but kept it from Wayne so as not to upset him. On August 9, 1988, the Oilers traded Gretzky, along with Marty McSorley and Mike Krushelnyski, to the Los Angeles Kings for Jimmy Carson, Martin Gelinas, $15 million in cash, and the Kings' first-round draft picks in 1989, 1991, and 1993. "The Trade" upset Canadians to such an extent that New Democratic Party House Leader Nelson Riis demanded that the government block it and Oilers owner Peter Pocklington was burned in effigy outside the Northlands Coliseum. Gretzky himself was considered a "traitor" by some Canadians for turning his back on his adopted hometown.

But Edmontonians generally bore no grudge against him. On his first appearance in Edmonton after the trade— a nationally televised game in Canada—he received a four-minute standing ovation. The Oilers' biggest crowd ever turned out. And after the 1988–89 season, a life-sized bronze statue of Gretzky was erected outside the Northlands Coliseum. He's depicted holding the Stanley Cup over his head.

● **In 1989,** Alexander Mogilny became the first Soviet front line player to defect to the NHL. He joined the Buffalo Sabres. Soviet officials called Mogilny's actions "disgusting." Within months, many more Soviet players would follow Mogilny's lead.

●**At the 1989** Entry Draft, Mats Sundin, a young Swedish star, became the first European player to be selected number one. He was taken by the Quebec Nordiques. Ten players named Jason were selected in the same draft, four of them in the first round.

● **In 1991,** the Vancouver Canucks signed 20-year-old Soviet phenom Pavel Bure to a four year, C$2.7-million contract and secured his release from the Central Red Army team in a Detroit courtroom. Bure, recognizing that the Canucks were willing to pay the Red Army only $200,000 of the $250,000 asking price for his transfer, agreed to fork over the remaining $50,000 out of his own pocket. Afraid they'd be considered cheapskates, the Canucks coughed up the extra fifty grand.

● **In October 1992,** Gil Stein was named interim NHL president after John Ziegler was dismissed for the way he'd handled the players' strike. Four months later, former NBA vice-president Gary Bettman was named the league's first-ever commissioner and took over from Stein, who was caught shamelessly promoting himself for a Hall of Fame berth.

⬤ **The 2004–05** NHL season would have been the 88th regular season of the NHL. The season was officially cancelled on February 16, 2005, due to an unresolved lockout that began on September 16, 2004. The loss of the 2004–05 season made the NHL the first North American professional sports league to cancel an entire season because of a labour dispute. It was also the first time the Stanley Cup was not awarded since 1919, when a Spanish flu pandemic caused the cancellation of the Stanley Cup finals.

⬤ **According to the IIHF,** 388 NHL players were signed by teams based in Europe at some point during the lockout, performing in 19 European leagues. Most of these players had a contract clause to return to the NHL when the league started up again.

⬤ **Key rule changes** that would dominate NHL hockey after the lockout were established at a meeting between the NHL and its top minor league, the American Hockey League. At the AHL's board of governors meeting in June 2004, the board, backed by the NHL, agreed to adopt new rules for the season. On July 5, 2004, the AHL publicly announced the 2004–05 rule changes, many of which had been passed as a result of the NHL's recommendations.

- In the case of a tie after overtime of regular season games, there is a shootout with five shots per team in the AHL and three shots per team in the NHL, and if the game is still tied, the shootout becomes sudden death.
- Goaltenders' leg pads were reduced in size from 30 centimetres (12 inches) to 27.5 centimetres (11 inches). This rule was postponed for a season, but by the resumption of the NHL, the leg pad rules were in effect.

- Goal lines were moved 0.6 metres (2 feet) closer to the end boards, from 3.35 metres (13 feet) to 3.96 metres (11 feet). The blue lines were moved to maintain an 18-metre (60-foot) attack zone in a 61-metre (200-foot) rink.
- During the first seven weeks of the 2004–05 AHL season, an experimental rule added a new trapezoid-shaped zone directly behind the net, restricting the area where a goaltender may play the puck. This rule was made official after the seven-week trial period.

These rule changes combined to make games shorter by 10 to 15 minutes per game, therefore "improving" the quality of the game by eliminating some downtime.

● **In the 2005–06** season, the NHL eliminated tie games and attempted to open up the game after the lockout. One of the most controversial changes was the league's zero-tolerance policy on obstruction penalties, cracking down on "clutching and grabbing." The changes led to more power plays and a sharp increase in scoring. Teams combined to score 6.1 goals per game in 2005–06, more than a full goal per game higher than in the 2003–04 season.

● **In the 2005–06** season, rookies Alexander Ovechkin and Sidney Crosby began their careers with the Washington Capitals and the Pittsburgh Penguins respectively. In their first three seasons, they each won both the Art Ross and Hart trophies; Crosby in 2007 and Ovechkin in 2008. Ovechkin added another Hart in 2009. The 2010 Hart Trophy winner was Henrik Sedin of the Vancouver Canucks.

● **In 2006–07,** Evgeni Malkin of the Pittsburgh Penguins became the first player in 89 years to score a goal in each of his first six games in the NHL. One of his teammates, forward Jordan Staal became the youngest player (18 years, 153 days) in NHL history to record a hat trick (on February 10, 2007). A third Penguin, 19-year-old phenom Sidney Crosby claimed the scoring title with 120 points, becoming the youngest player in NHL history to achieve the feat. Crosby scored a goal against the Carolina Hurricanes to pass Wayne Gretzky as the youngest player (19 years, 207 days) in NHL history to reach 200 career points.

● **The NHL's** 90th season opened on September 29, 2007, with the first of back-to-back games in London, England at The O_2. They were the first NHL regular season games ever played in Europe. Both games featured the defending Stanley Cup Champion Anaheim Ducks and the Los Angeles Kings (who are owned by the same company that owns The O_2). The average attendance was 17,625 per game.

● **The first outdoor game** in over four years featuring the Pittsburgh Penguins and the Buffalo Sabres was played in Buffalo on January 1, 2008. It was the first time an NHL regular-season game had been played outdoors in the United States, and it set an NHL attendance record of 71,217 people. The only previous outdoor NHL game was the Heritage Classic played between the Montreal Canadiens and the Edmonton Oilers at Commonwealth Stadium in Edmonton on November 22, 2003.

● **Many of the NHL's** top players participated in the 2010 Winter Olympics in Vancouver. The Olympic men's hockey tournament ran from February 16 to 28, 2010. It was the first time that the Winter Olympics were held in an NHL market, as well as the first time an NHL-sized rink was used (as opposed to the bigger one normally employed for international play). The Canadians won gold, the Americans captured silver, and the Finnish team won bronze. At the end of the tournament, United States goaltender Ryan Miller was named Tournament MVP. In order to make way for the Olympics, the Vancouver Canucks endured the longest road trip in NHL history, playing 14 straight road games from January 27 to March 13, 2010

The NHL's Fascinating Past TWO

From 1917 to 1929, the National Hockey League, successor to the National Hockey Association, grew into a thriving 10-team international circuit. It was the Golden Age of Sports and many famous players made their professional debuts, notably Howie Morenz, King Clancy, Eddie Shore, and the Cook brothers. Other famous stars, such as Fred "Cyclone" Taylor, Bad Joe Hall, Georges Vezina, and Joe Malone, were at the end of the hockey highway.

Forming a new league in 1917 wasn't easy. Only a handful of teams were interested in joining. And when you start out with four teams and one drops out after the first two weeks, it's a stretch to call it a league.

The NHL had a wobbly beginning. The first year of play gave no indication that the league would be around for generations. The Montreal Wanderers won their first home game over Toronto by a margin of 10–9. It was wartime, and soldiers in uniform were invited to fill the many empty seats for the opener. Little did the Wanderers know that their first victory would also be their last. A few days later, Montreal's Westmount Arena burned to the ground, forcing the Wanderers (with a 1–5 record and 35 goals against) to withdraw from the circuit. Prior to the season, the Quebec franchise had decided not to ice a team, so there were only three teams—the Canadiens, Ottawa, and Toronto—left in competition.

● **The Canadiens** won their opener over Ottawa 7–4 with Joe Malone scoring five goals for the Habs.

On the eve of the NHL opener in Montreal, the owner of the Montreal arena said he was fed up with the poor calibre of hockey displayed by the two NHL clubs based there—the Canadiens and Wanderers—and threatened to turf them both from his rink and reserve the ice for pleasure skating if the teams didn't shape up.

● **When Ottawa's** starters skated out for an away game against Toronto in January, the Senators bench was empty—they had no substitutes on hand. Toronto reciprocated by emptying its own bench. It was the only NHL game ever played with the minimum of 12 players involved.

● **Later that month,** Bad Joe Hall of Montreal and Alf Skinner of Toronto tried to decapitate each other in a vicious stick-swinging duel. Both were arrested and hauled into court, where a lenient judge released them with suspended sentences.

● **Two Toronto stars,** Harry Cameron and Reg Noble, were fined $100 each by management after they refused to play in a game at Montreal in February. They had also been caught breaking training.

● **Toronto and Montreal** were tied in the standings and met in a two-game, total-goals to count playoff. Toronto won the league championship, 10 goals to 7. Both games were described as slugfests. Toronto went on to capture the

Stanley Cup over Vancouver, the champions of the Pacific Coast Hockey Association, winning three games to two on home ice. The westerners wore very little padding and were pounded by the more aggressive Blueshirts. Although the Blueshirts, soon to be known as the Arenas, had won the Stanley Cup in 1914, they became the first NHL club to win the Stanley Cup.

● **During the 1918** season, Ken Randall of Toronto owed the NHL $35 in fines. Pay up before the next game or you won't play, he was told. Randall produced $32 in bills and 300 pennies. When a league official refused to accept the pennies, Randall placed them in a neat pile on the ice. A teammate skated by and whacked the pile with his stick, scattering pennies in all directions. The Toronto players were forced to scoop them up while Randall borrowed suitable folding money to pay the rest of his fine.

● **During the first** season of play in the NHL (1917–18), three players who scored 20 or more goals set goals-per-game averages that have never been topped. Montreal's Joe Malone, with 44 goals in 20 games, averaged 2.20 goals per game. Cy Denneny (Ottawa), with 36 goals in 20 games, finished in second place with a 1.80 average. Newsy Lalonde (Montreal) scored 23 goals in 14 games, an average of 1.64. No modern-day player has come close to those averages. In 1983–84, Wayne Gretzky averaged 1.18 goals per game.

● **Here's a tale** of one of hockey's strangest goals—one that should never have counted. Former NHL all-star Jack Adams was the man who scored it. In 1920–21, Adams starred for the famed Vancouver Millionaires. In the final game of the 1920–21 season, Vancouver beat Victoria 11–8.

During that high-scoring affair, Adams accidentally scored a goal—on his own goaltender! It turned out to be the most bizarre of goals because the official scorer credited Adams for the goal and it was added to his total in the individual scoring race. Have you ever heard of such a thing? Why he got credit for the goal has never been made clear. But he did. In fact, the bizarre goal vaulted him into fifth place in the individual scoring race.

● **In March 1923,** a teenage reporter with the *Toronto Star* was assigned to broadcast a hockey game at Mutual Street Arena in Toronto. Sitting at rinkside, Foster Hewitt called the game between the Parkdale Canoe Club and Kitchener on the *Star*'s new radio station, CFCA. It was the beginning of a career that would make the Hewitt voice the most recognized in Canada.

● **In the spring** of 1923, the Ottawa Senators journeyed to Vancouver, where they faced two challengers for the Stanley Cup. Ottawa ousted the Vancouver Millionaires in four games in the first series, and then captured the Cup with two straight wins over the Edmonton Eskimos, who were standing by. In one of the games against Edmonton, Ottawa's King Clancy played every position for his team, including that of goaltender. In 1923, a goaltender who took a penalty had to sit in the penalty box. When Clint Benedict, the Ottawa goalie, was penalized, Clancy took over in net for two minutes and was not scored upon.

● **In 1924–25,** the NHL added two new franchises: the Boston Bruins and Montreal Maroons. The entrance fee was $15,000. They joined the Hamilton Tigers, Toronto St. Pats, Montreal Canadiens, and Ottawa Senators. The

24-game schedule was beefed up to 30 games, and the six extra games brought pay hikes to players on three of the four existing clubs. The cheapskate Hamilton Tigers refused to compensate their players for the extra workload, even though the Tigers finished atop the NHL standings and earned a bye into the NHL finals.

● **After a season-ending** loss to Montreal on March 9, the Tigers held a team meeting on the train headed back to Hamilton. They decided not to suit up for another game until each man was paid a total of $200 for the six extra games they'd played.

"We're officially on strike," player Red Green told reporters. "We don't care about the playoffs and the Stanley Cup."

The player revolt—the first strike of a professional sports team—became front page news. NHL president Frank Calder immediately suspended the Tigers, fined each man $200, and stated that the winner of the Montreal–Toronto series would compete against the western champions in the Stanley Cup finals (Montreal would lose to Victoria).

The player revolt cost the Tigers a chance for the Cup. And they never got another one. Before the next season rolled around, Big Bill Dwyer—a New York bootlegger—purchased the Hamilton franchise for $75,000. The franchise was moved to Madison Square Garden and renamed the New York Americans.

● **It's surprising the NHL** would welcome a new owner like Big Bill Dwyer. He dominated bootlegging in New York. Partnered with notorious criminals, he ran illegal bootlegging operations that stretched from Europe to New York. He bribed politicians, police, and Coast Guard officials to assure there'd be no interference.

He not only owned the Americans, but later he secretly owned the Pittsburgh Pirates, although the NHL would list boxer Benny Leonard as the owner.

Dwyer often tried to rig NHL games by hiring dishonest pals as goal judges. They were instructed to flash the red light if the puck came anywhere close to the opposing team's goal line.

He was the first NHL owner—but not the last—to serve jail time: a two-year sentence for attempting to bribe members of the Coast Guard.

● **In 1926,** the New York Rangers, Chicago Black Hawks, and Detroit Cougars (later renamed the Red Wings) joined the NHL. The Western Hockey League disbanded and sold most of its players to the new NHL teams, leaving the NHL as the undisputed top hockey league in North America.

● **Did I mention** the NHL had a wobbly beginning? Well, it was still in turmoil throughout the thirties and into the forties. For the 1930–31 season, the Detroit Cougars changed their name to the Falcons and the Pittsburgh franchise was transferred to Philadelphia, where they were called the Quakers. They didn't stay around long, dropping out after one season. Ottawa folded prior to the 1931–32 season but jumped back in the following year. There was another name change for the Detroit franchise in 1932, with the Red Wings supplanting the Falcons. Ottawa had financial problems in 1934 and moved to St. Louis, where they became the Eagles. But the Eagles folded their wings after one season. The Montreal Maroons played their final game on March 17, 1938. In 1941–42, the New York Americans adopted the name Brooklyn Americans, but it didn't help attendance. The Americans bowed out in 1942.

● **In 1932,** NHL owners decided to introduce a cap on players' salaries. It was decided that no player would earn more than $7,500 per season.

● **In the 1930s,** curved blue lines were suggested as a cure for offsides. Blue lines curving in toward the defensive zone near the side boards were designed to permit wingers to take a quick pass from their centremen without breaking stride and going offside. It's not known if the idea ever made it past the drawing board.

● **In December 1932,** a raging blizzard swept through Chicago, where the championship of the pro football league was about to be decided. The Chicago Bears would meet the Portsmouth (Ohio) Spartans in the first NFL title game. What to do? Officials decided to move the game indoors— into the cavernous Chicago Stadium, a hockey rink. The seats were moved back and several inches of dirt were spread over the cement floor. Because the field was only 80 yards long, every time a team crossed midfield it was penalized 20 yards. Despite the atrocious weather, 11,000 fans turned out. Only one touchdown was scored—by the Bears' Red Grange, one of the greatest players in history. The Bears won 9–0.

● **Visible time** clocks were first introduced in NHL arenas in 1933–34.

● **For the 1934–35** season, the NHL adopted the penalty shot rule. A player tripped while in the clear and prevented from scoring a goal was awarded a free shot, taken from within a 10-foot circle situated 38 feet from the goal. Detroit player Ralph "Scotty" Bowman scored the first penalty shot goal against the Montreal Maroons' Alec Connell.

● **In 1937,** the New York Rangers were forced to play all but one game of the best-of-five finals against the Red Wings on Detroit ice. The circus had forced the Rangers out of Madison Square Garden. Red Wings goaltender Earl Robertson, who never played a regular season game for the Wings during his career, set a record for rookie netminders when he blanked the Rangers twice in the final two games of the series.

I was happy to get out of New York that year. I didn't want a circus elephant stepping on me.

● **The first telecast** of a hockey game occurred on October 29, 1938 when the 2nd and 3rd periods of a game from Harringay Arena in London, England were aired.

The first telecast of an NHL game took place at Madison Square Garden in New York on February 25, 1940. Not many fans witnessed the telecast between the Rangers and the Canadiens because there were only 300 TV sets scattered throughout New York at the time, and their screens were only seven inches wide.

● **In 1942,** manager Jack Adams of Detroit, with his team leading Toronto 3–1 in games, jumped on the ice at the end of game four of the Stanley Cup finals and tried to rough up the referee. It marked a turning point in the series. Adams was suspended indefinitely and his team sagged. Toronto won four games in a row and captured the Stanley Cup in what has been called hockey's greatest comeback.

● **Prior to the 1941–42** season, the NHL introduced two types of penalty shots: A minor penalty shot was taken from a line 28 feet out from the goal. A major penalty shot, awarded when a player was tripped from behind on a breakaway, allowed the shooter to skate right in on goal.

Did you hear the one about the hockey player who took a penalty shot and passed the puck instead of shooting? That's a joke, folks. It never happened.

● **During the 1941–42** season, in Boston, announcements were made over the public address system during game intermissions, pleading with fans to return the pucks that were shot or deflected into the stands. "We need them returned because of a wartime shortage of rubber."

● **Military obligations** continued to cut talent from NHL rosters during the 1943–44 campaign. The Stanley Cup champion Detroit Red Wings lost nine starters to military service, while the already badly depleted New York Rangers lost five more players, including top scorer Lynn Patrick. The Rangers suffered through a horrendous 6–39–5 season, allowing a then record 310 goals in just 50 games. Goaltender Ken "Tubby" McAuley endured a 6.24 goals-against average, still the highest mark in NHL history for anyone who has appeared in at least 30 games.

● **Jackie Hamilton** of the Leafs was awarded a major penalty shot one night, skated in, and scored. But the opposing team argued the shot should have been for a minor penalty. The referee agreed and ordered Hamilton to try again—this time from 28 feet out. Jackie took a second shot—and scored again. But only one of his scoring shots counted.

● **On New Year's Day,** 1943, Reg Bentley from Delisle, Saskatchewan, joined his younger brothers Max and Doug on the Chicago Black Hawks. It was the first time in NHL history that three brothers played on the same line. Two days later, Reg scored his first—and only—NHL goal with his two brothers assisting. It was another first—the only time three brothers teamed up for a goal. By the way, the record for most brothers to play in the NHL is six—the Sutter brothers from Viking, Alberta. And it could have been seven. Gary Sutter, said to be the best of the players in this amazing family, stayed home to work on the farm.

● **The national anthem** of the home team has been played before NHL games since the 1946–47 season. I wanted to sing it one night, but they said my voice was too squeaky. A player told me once the anthem was a jinx. He said, "Pete, every time they play that song, I have a bad game." That's another joke, folks.

● **Betting on games** is a no-no in the NHL. On March 9, 1948, NHL president Clarence Campbell suspended for life New York Ranger Billy Taylor and Boston Bruin Don Gallinger for gambling violations. The suspensions were lifted in 1970, when both players were middle-aged.

● **In October 1947,** the first annual All-Star Game was played in Toronto. The Cup-holding Leafs faced a team of All-Stars coached by Montreal's Dick Irvin. The All-Stars won 4–3, but the game was marred when Bill Mosienko of Chicago suffered a broken leg.

● **Protective glass** surrounding the boards of the rink first appeared in Toronto's Maple Leaf Gardens in 1948 and soon became mandatory in all NHL buildings. Now that was a good idea.

● **In 1949,** the ice in most NHL arenas was dull grey. Some bright individual, noting that televised games were on the horizon, suggested that white ice might be a major improvement. It was a great idea. Arena floors were painted white and everyone gasped at how much better they could follow me—the bouncing puck.

● **In the spring** of 1951, Toronto defenceman Bill Barilko scored a dramatic Stanley Cup–winning overtime goal in game five of the finals versus Montreal. All of the final games went to overtime. Sadly, Barilko died a few months after the playoffs in a plane crash in the Northern Ontario bush.

● **Televised hockey** began in Canada in the 1952–53 season. The black and white broadcast started at 9:30 p.m., so viewers missed all of the first period and some of the second. It's said that Leaf forward Bob Hassard scored the first goal ever seen on the English version of *Hockey Night in Canada*.

● **In 1952–53,** the NHL almost adopted a seventh team. On May 14, the Cleveland Barons' application was accepted, provided the team deposit $450,000 in a show of good faith and it had sufficient working capital to consort with the six established teams. Delighted that he was able to meet all the stipulations, owner Jim Hendy showed up at the June meetings, only to be informed that the league still had some concerns. Try again next year, he was told.

● **In 1955–56,** Red Kelly of Detroit, noted for his clean, sportsmanlike play, was involved in a fight with Eric Nesterenko of the Toronto Maple Leafs. It was a ding-dong battle, and Kelly, besides a minor and two majors, received a misconduct. He took more penalty minutes in one skirmish than he'd received in the previous eight seasons.

● **On March 10, 1955,** a strange-looking machine rolled onto the rink at the Montreal Forum and began making fresh ice. The vehicle was called a Zamboni after its inventor, Frank Zamboni of California. Before that, arena workers had pulled barrels of water mounted on wheels around the ice. For a time, Zamboni's machine was known simply as "the ice machine." Then one night at a hockey game, some leather-lunged fan yelled out, "Get the Zamboni out and make some new ice!" Others took up the chant, and from then on the Zamboni name became part of hockey.

● **In 1955,** scoreboards showing scores from out-of-town games became mandatory, beginning in all NHL arenas. It was another good idea. Teams in a playoff race want to know what's happening around the league.

● **The Montreal Canadiens** captured five straight Stanley Cups from 1956 to 1960—a playoff record. But the record might easily have been six if star player Rocket Richard hadn't been sitting on the sidelines in the spring of 1955.

NHL president Clarence Campbell had suspended Rocket Richard, the Canadiens' greatest star, for an attack on Bruins defenceman Hal Laycoe and for striking a game official during a melee at the Boston Garden. The harsh penalty kept Richard out of the remaining regular season games and all playoff games that spring. Montreal fans were furious. The next game at the Forum—against Detroit on March 17, 1955—would begin on time. But it would never finish.

The fans were in an ugly mood, and their anger and frustration deepened when the Red Wings slapped in four fast goals in the opening period. The Canadiens, holding a four-point lead over Detroit prior to the game, could see their lead and the league championship slipping away. And Richard's chance to win his first individual scoring crown was in jeopardy as well.

Late in the first period, Campbell slipped into the Forum and took his seat. The fans immediately hurled verbal taunts and slurs at the man who'd suspended their hero. A thug rushed up to Campbell and held out his hand, as if to offer his support. Then he drew his arm back and punched the league president. Another fan squeezed a ripe tomato over Campbell's head.

Police rushed to the scene and rescued the president. Then a tear gas bomb exploded on the ice. Fans began choking from the fumes. The fire marshal ordered an evacuation of the arena and people fled toward the exits. The game was cancelled and forfeited to Detroit.

Outside the Forum, a large crowd went on a rampage. Vandals threw rocks through the windows of the arena. Then a howling mob surged down St. Catherine Street, smashing windows, looting shops, and setting fires.

The forfeited game added two points to the Detroit total, and when they beat Montreal in the final game of the season a few nights later, the Red Wings captured the league title (by two points) for the seventh consecutive season.

Rocket Richard was deprived of winning his first scoring crown when teammate Boom Boom Geoffrion edged him out by a single point, 75–74. For this, Geoffrion was booed by his own fans.

When Detroit and Montreal met in the finals, the series went the full seven games. Detroit won the deciding game 3–1 at the Detroit Olympia. But it might have been a different story if the Rocket hadn't been fuming on the sidelines.

● **In 1956–57,** the Leafs unveiled a prize rookie, Frank Mahovlich, a 19-year-old who could play centre or left wing. In his first game against Montreal, Frank was told to keep an eye on Montreal's superstar, Rocket Richard.

"Did you keep an eye on him?" I asked.

"I did, Pete," he told me. "I grabbed him around the waist and held on. Then he glared at me and said, 'Kid, let go.'"

"What did you do?"

"I let him go."

● **A minimum salary** of $7,000 was first introduced in the NHL prior to the 1958–59 season. And many players were happy to get it. There was no salary cap at the time, but hockey players made far less than pro athletes in other sports. Most of today's players make more than $7,000 per game. Some of them earn $7,000 per period.

● **The 1958–59** season is one the New York Rangers would rather forget. On February 1, the Rangers downed the Red Wings 5–4 in New York. Ranger defenceman Lou Fontinato was incensed when he witnessed Gordie Howe clubbing Eddie Shack over the ear with his stick, and he raced in to challenge Howe. Big mistake. Howe scored with a wicked punch that all but terminated the fight. His uppercut broke Fontinato's nose and left it several degrees off centre.

On February 15, at Madison Square Garden, jovial goalie Gump Worsley was working on a 1–0 shutout over Montreal with 10 minutes left to play. Then the Canadiens scored five goals to win 5–1. Ranger coach Phil Watson blew a gasket in the dressing room. Livid with rage, he screamed obscenities at his Ranger players and ordered them back on the ice for an hour-long workout. Watson said Worsley was excused; he hadn't played badly. "It's better than fining them all," general manager Muzz Patrick said of the unusual post-game workout.

With five games left in the season, the Rangers had a seven-point lead over Punch Imlach's Toronto Maple Leafs. Then the Rangers went into a nosedive and the Leafs picked up the pace. A key game was played on March 19 between Toronto and the Canadiens. Goalie Jacques Plante couldn't play due to a problem with boils, so the Canadiens used Claude Pronovost in goal. He was dreadful and was bombed for five goals before coach Toe Blake yanked him in the third period. Claude Cyr took over. It was his first and last NHL game. Toronto won 6–3. On March 22, the Canadiens called up the reliable Charlie Hodge from the Montreal Royals. Too bad for the Rangers. Hodge beat them 4–2. The Rangers still had a slim chance to make the playoffs if Detroit beat Toronto. The Red Wings jumped into a 2–0 lead, then fell apart and the Leafs won 6–4, The Rangers were out, the Leafs were in.

● **In 1958,** the Boston Bruins called up a fast-skating forward from the minor league Quebec Aces and Maritimer Willie O'Ree became the first black player in the NHL. His major league salary was $3,500, and he was subjected to racial slurs around the league. What wasn't generally known was that O'Ree was blind in one eye, the result of a high stick accident in junior hockey. Yet he played for 20 seasons, mostly in the minor leagues. During his 45 games with the Bruins, played over two seasons, he scored four goals and 10 assists. On April 7, 2010, O'Ree received the Order of Canada, the highest civilian award for a Canadian citizen. He was honoured as a pioneer of hockey and dedicated mentor to kids in Canada and the U.S.

● **In 1961–62,** Red Kelly announced that he would seek the Liberal nomination for the federal riding of York West. But he didn't plan to give up his hockey career. He won the nomination and the riding and became a member of Parliament after defeating hockey agent Alan Eagleson in the 1962 federal election.

● **In 1967–68,** a new era began in the NHL. The league doubled in size, bringing six new cities into the fold. The expansion brought in the Philadelphia Flyers, St. Louis Blues, Los Angeles Kings, Minnesota North Stars, California Seals, and Pittsburgh Penguins. Canadian fans were irate that no Canadian teams were added, particularly since Vancouver had been considered a lock. The Vancouver bid was reportedly very weak, but Montreal and Toronto were not interested in sharing *Hockey Night in Canada* TV revenues with another Canadian club. And Chicago's support for expansion was contingent on the creation of a St. Louis franchise, though no formal bid had actually been received from St. Louis. The new franchise holder was forced to purchase the decrepit St. Louis Arena, which James Norris, the boss of the Black Hawks, owned.

● **During the 1967–68** season, the NHL board of governors turned down a suggestion that players wear their names on the back of their jerseys. That seems like a bonehead decision. Perhaps they were afraid fans wouldn't buy their overpriced programs that listed all the players' names and numbers.

● **On October 11, 1967,** the St. Louis Blues, an expansion team, opened at home with great fanfare. Orchestra leader Guy Lombardo and his Royal Canadians played at rinkside while TV personality Arthur Godfrey skated a duet with figure skating queen Aja Zanova. Seth Martin, a 34-year-old former amateur netminder who'd starred at the World Championships for Canada, tended goal for the Blues.

● **How's this** for an iron man streak? From March 8, 1952, to October 18, 1967, Andy Hebenton played 1,062 consecutive games with the Portland Buckaroos before ending his streak to attend his father's funeral. The streak included 216 games in the WHA, 630 games in the NHL, and another 216 games back in the WHA.

● **The Buffalo Sabres** and the Vancouver Canucks joined the NHL in 1970–71 after paying the $6-million entrance fee.

● **In 1970–71,** goaltender Ken Dryden, a former star at Cornell, broke into pro hockey with the Montreal Canadiens' farm team in Halifax. His older brother, Dave, was also a goalie, then with the Buffalo Sabres.

Late in the 1970–71 season, the Habs brought Dryden up to the NHL and coach Al MacNeil gave him half a dozen starts. People were surprised when he won every game he played in. One night at the Montreal Forum, on March 20, 1971, he and his brother made hockey history when they played against each other. That night, Ken Dryden's Habs beat Dave Dryden's Sabres 5–2.

● **In the 1979–80** season, it became mandatory for all players entering the league to wear helmets. The last player to perform without one was Craig MacTavish of the Edmonton Oilers. It took players a long time to wise up. I guess they'd become used to getting knocked on the noggin.

● **Prior to the 1982–83** season, the NHL's first civil law suit resulting from an on-ice incident ended with plaintiff Dennis Polonich receiving an award of $850,000 from a U.S. federal court jury. Polonich, a former Red Wing player, had sued for damages for an injury he'd suffered at the Detroit Olympia on October 25, 1978, when he was struck in the face by a stick wielded by Wilf Paiement, then with the Colorado Rockies. The case was only the third of its kind in major league sports.

⬤**In 1982,** the L. A. Kings made history when they drafted 27-year-old Viktor Nechayev, a Soviet player from Siberia. Nechayev had met and married a Yale University student and lived in the United States. On Oct. 17, 1982, he scored the first NHL goal by a Russian-trained player. After three games, he was shipped to the minors. He refused to report and retired from hockey.

⬤**During the 1982–83** season, Bill Hunter, an Edmonton promoter, proposed to purchase the St. Louis Blues and move them to Saskatoon. But the deal never went through. Don Cherry was said to be Hunter's choice as coach of the Saskatoon team.

⬤**In the spring** of 1983, the New York Islanders defeated the Edmonton Oilers in four straight games to win their fourth consecutive Stanley Cup. One year later, the Isles were unable to match Montreal's record of five consecutive Cup wins when they lost (in five games) to the Oilers in the 1984 finals.

⬤ **The New Jersey Devils** once played before a home crowd of 334. On January 22, 1987, a blizzard dropped 38 centimetres (15 inches) of snow on the Meadowlands, home of the Devils. The game with Calgary was delayed 106 minutes because only 13 Devils had made it to the arena by game time. Even so, the Devils defeated the Flames 7–5.

⬤ **In 1987,** the NHL made bench-clearing brawls a thing of the past by introducing strict new rules. The first player to leave his team's bench and join in a fight would face a 10-game suspension. What's more, his team would be fined $10,000 and his coach would be suspended for five games.

● **At the 2000** All-Star Game in Toronto, the NHL announced that the entire league would retire Wayne Gretzky's famous number 99—a first in all of professional sports. Someone asked me recently when I would retire, and I told him, "Peter Puck will never retire. I'll be around as long as hockey is played."

● **Perhaps Montreal's** biggest blunder in hockey was at the draft table. In June 1980, the Habs, with first pick in the Entry Draft, chose Regina's Doug Wickenheiser over hometown favourite Denis Savard, an immensely skilled francophone. Savard had scored 63 goals and 181 points for the junior Canadiens in his final season. He was said to be the logical heir to legendary scorers like Guy Lafleur and Henri Richard. With second choice, the Winnipeg Jets took David Babych, and Chicago, drafting third, grabbed Savard. He went on to an illustrious Hall of Fame career as a Black Hawk.

The Canadiens traded for Savard in 1990, when his best seasons were behind him. But they gave up Chris Chelios, a great defenceman, in the deal. Commentator Don Cherry was astounded. "Chelios is 28 and at his best in the clutch. Savard is almost 30. Are you kiddin' me? I'll say this. If Chelios's name had been Tremblay, the deal would never have happened."

● **Chicago Blackhawks** general manager Bob Pulford was asked one day, "Are you going to draft Bobby Hull's son Brett? Someday he may fill your arena."

"No. The kid's too slow."

"How about Doug Gilmour, who led the OHA in scoring?"

"No, the kid's too small."

Brett Hull went on to score 741 goals in the NHL and was inducted into the Hockey Hall of Fame in 2009. Gilmour scored 450 goals in the NHL. And it was a Chicago scout who told me about another kid named Gretzky, "Pete, the kid's too slow and too small. He'll never play in the NHL."

● **In 1991,** the NHL introduced video replay—and about time, too. Fans could see in slow motion whether or not I crossed the goalie's red line.

● **The Ottawa Senators,** who were accused of throwing the final game of the 1992–93 season in order to get first pick in the Entry Draft (Alexandre Daigle), were slapped with a $100,000 fine by NHL commissioner Gary Bettman. The hanky panky was all for naught. Daigle never became the star Ottawa thought he would be.

● **In 1994,** the New York Rangers ended a 54-year drought by winning the Stanley Cup on home ice with a stirring seven-game victory over the Vancouver Canucks. Rangers defenceman Brian Leetch led all playoff scorers with 34 points in 23 games and became the first U.S.-born player to capture the Conn Smythe Trophy as playoff MVP.

● **In 1993,** the Tampa Bay Lightning set an indoor attendance record of 27,227 when they played the Florida Panthers in a huge arena called the Thunderdome. The Lightning playing in the Thunderdome? Lightning and Thunder. Now there's a match.

● **On November 22, 2003,** the largest crowd in NHL history—57,167—showed up at Edmonton's Commonwealth Stadium for an outdoor game called the Heritage Classic between the hometown Oilers and the Montreal Canadiens. The Habs beat the Oilers 4–3.

● **In 2009,** when the Pittsburgh Penguins bounced back to defeat Detroit for the Stanley Cup, they became just the second team, after the 1971 Montreal Canadiens, to win the championship after losing the first two games of the series on the road.

● **The outdoor record** for a hockey game was broken in May 2010 when the U.S. team faced Germany in the opener of the IIHF World Championships. A crowd of 77,803 filled the Veltins Arena in Gelsenkirchen, Germany.

● **The Pittsburgh Penguins'** victory over Detroit in the 2009 Stanley Cup finals, coupled with the Pittsburgh Steelers' triumph in the Super Bowl four months earlier, gave Pittsburgh the distinction of being the only city to win a Super Bowl and a Stanley Cup in the same year.

Those Cool, Courageous Goalies

I love hockey's goaltenders, even though they often get angry with me when I dare to enter their nets. And they are very clever at keeping me out. Most of them are cool and unflappable. I admire their courage. If someone blasted pucks at me at 100 miles per hour, I think I'd scamper in behind the net and cover my eyes.

● **One of the braves**t—and most overworked—goalies was Ed Johnston of the Boston Bruins. On March 22, 1964, Johnston became the last goaltender in NHL history to play every minute of every game for the entire season. He finished the season with a record of 18–40–12.

● **Did you know** that for the first 40 years of NHL play, goalies didn't wear face masks? How brave is that? And don't you admire the fabulous artwork on their masks? Years ago, goalie Doug Favell of the Philadelphia Flyers painted his mask bright orange. It looked like a pumpkin. Gerry Cheevers of the Boston Bruins had stitches painted on his mask to indicate where flying pucks or sticks would have cut him had he not been wearing it. Gilles Gratton, when he played for the Rangers, had a lion with big teeth painted on his mask. Gratton would often growl at incoming forwards, pretending he was king of the jungle.

⬤ **Some goaltenders** in the league's early years would wear caps or hats on their heads, not only to keep their heads warm but also to protect themselves from young lads with peashooters who stood behind them in the crowd. The young fans tried to distract the goalies by shooting peas at them through the chicken-wire screen at the end of the rink.

Come to think of it, what ever happened to peashooters? Most of them disappeared decades ago—and a good thing, too. If you don't know what peashooters are, ask your grandparents or check the Internet.

⬤ **In hockey's** early days, a goalkeeper who deliberately fell to the ice to stop a shot with his body was subject to a $2 fine. Every goalie was expected to be a stand-up guy.

⬤ **Pioneer goaltenders** wore ordinary shin pads. In 1896, Whitey Merritt of the Winnipeg Victorias began using white cricket pads to protect his shins, and his bright idea was quickly adopted by all goalies. In the early years, protection for the groin area was provided by a thick glove or winter mitt stuffed down the front of the trousers.

Ouch!

⬤ **In 1898,** Fred Chittick, the goaltender for the Ottawa team, decided not to suit up for a game when the team manager refused to allot him a large number of complimentary tickets for a big game.

⬤ **A goalie named** Fred Brophy of Montreal Westmount made hockey history in 1905 when he rushed down the ice and slapped the puck past a stunned Paddy Moran, the netminder for Quebec. Nobody had seen a goalie score a goal before. Brophy was so proud of his feat that he did it again the following season.

● **Georges Vezina,** after whom the Vezina Trophy is named, didn't learn how to skate until he was a teenager. Growing up, he played in goal wearing shoes or boots. Joining the Montreal Canadiens for the 1910–11 NHA season, Vezina went on to become one of the greatest goalies in NHA and NHL history. By then wearing skates, he earned the most unusual nickname in hockey: the "Chicoutimi Cucumber." Why? Because he was from Chicoutimi, Quebec, and he was said to be as cool as a cucumber between the pipes. Vezina never missed a league or playoff game until he left a game against Pittsburgh after one period on the night of November 28, 1925. Suffering from tuberculosis, he died four months later.

● **On February 18, 1928,** goalie Alec Connell of the Ottawa Senators recorded his sixth consecutive shutout with a 1–0 win over the Montreal Canadiens. Connell's mark has never been surpassed.

● **During the 1928–29** season, Canadiens goaltender George Hainsworth recorded an astonishing number of shutouts—22 in 44 games. It's another record that has never been equalled. Hainsworth is third on the list of goalies with most career shutouts with 94. Terry Sawchuk is second with 103, Martin Brodeur first with 110 after the 2009–10 season. And Marty's not through yet.

● **Get this, fans.** Goalie Percy LeSueur used the same goal stick in all league and playoff games for five consecutive seasons. The battered stick is on display at the Hockey

Hall of Fame in Toronto. Today's goalies will use dozens of sticks in a single season. "Peerless" Percy played on Stanley Cup winners with the Ottawa Senators in 1909 and 1911 and served as captain for three seasons. His career spanned 50 years as a player, coach, manager, referee, broadcaster, and columnist. He is also credited with inventing the gauntlet-style gloves worn by goaltenders.

● **During the 1936** Winter Olympic Games in Germany, Japanese goaltender Teiji Honma surprised spectators when he donned a face mask during the competition. That

was the year Great Britain won the gold medal in hockey when 11 players who were born in England but raised in Canada led the Brits to their only Olympic hockey title.

● **On December 1, 1938,** Boston rookie Frank Brimsek set a record for freshman goalies with six shutouts in his first eight games. It was an amazing start to a Hall of Fame career.

● **Goalie Bill Durnan** didn't make the NHL until 1943, when he was 27 years old. He played only seven seasons, but he established several records. He was the first goalie to win the Vezina Trophy for four straight years, and he captured it six times in seven years. He was a First Team All-Star for six of his seven seasons. When he was young, Durnan learned how to switch his goal stick from hand to hand, making him ambidextrous. Incoming forwards didn't know what to expect. The new trapper-style goal gloves in use today prevent goalies from switching the stick from hand to hand.

● **After retiring** from pro hockey in 1942, goalie Moe Roberts made a brief comeback in 1945–46, playing 24 games with a minor league club, and later became a trainer for the Black Hawks. On November 24, 1951, Roberts strapped on the pads for one period of hockey in Chicago's 6–2 win over Detroit. He was almost 46 years old and had last played in the NHL in 1933–34.

● **The Leafs' Johnny Bower,** who liked to keep his age a secret, was the oldest goalie ever to play in a Stanley Cup playoff series. He was 44 years, 5 months and 28 days old when he tended goal for the Leafs in 1969. He retired in 1971, four months after his 46th birthday.

● **Goalie Al Rollins** had a terrific season for the Chicago Black Hawks in 1953–54. Even though his team finished dead last in the standings, at season's end Rollins was awarded the Hart Trophy as the NHL's most valuable player. Amazingly, the All-Star selectors overlooked Rollins that season. They placed Toronto's Harry Lumley on the first team and Terry Sawchuk on the second.

Peter Puck wants to know how a player can be voted best in the league and not be an All-Star.

● **In 1959,** Hall of Fame goalie Jacques Plante made the goalie mask a vital piece of goaltending equipment. Plante, star goalie with the Canadiens for many years, wore a homemade mask he devised after he suffered a gash on his nose during a game in New York. Many years earlier, in 1930, goalie Clint Benedict of the Ottawa Senators stopped a Howie Morenz shot with his nose and immediately asked a Boston manufacturer to create a mask. The mask, made of leather, covered the nose but made it difficult for Benedict to see pucks at his feet, so he discarded it and soon after retired from hockey.

● **Goalie Glenn Hall's** amazing "iron man" record came to an end in November 1962 when he left the Chicago net suffering from back pain. Hall, who played without a mask for much of his career, participated in 502 consecutive regular season games (551, counting playoffs).

I felt sorry for Hall. He was so stressed out that he threw up before every game—and sometimes between periods. That couldn't have been much fun. When Dennis Hull joined the Hawks as a rookie, he asked Hall, "Do you always throw up before each game?" The veteran growled, "No, just since you joined the team." Now that's funny!

⬤ **On January 27,** 1963, Montreal goalie Jacques Plante complained that the goal posts in the Chicago Stadium were not tall enough. A measurement proved that Plante had keen eyesight. The posts were only 3 feet 10 inches instead of the regulation 4 feet high.

⬤ **When netminder** Gary Smith was traded from Chicago to Vancouver in 1973, he announced to a press gathering, "Everything you've heard about me is true. I'm a fantastic goaltender."

Smith was a bit of a flake. In his first NHL game, with Toronto during the 1965–66 season, he raced up the ice and tried to score a goal, only to be flattened at the Montreal blue line by J. C. Tremblay.

In another game, he punted me high in the air, so high I almost hit the clock.

● **The Toronto Maple Leafs** won their last Stanley Cup in 1967 with a 3–1 triumph over the Montreal Canadiens at Maple Leaf Gardens. Toronto fans who witnessed the Leafs topple the Habs four games to two in the final series haven't seen Lord Stanley's old chalice since.

It was goaltender Terry Sawchuk who was largely responsible for ending the series in game six and who admitted afterward, "This was the greatest thrill of my life."

The game's first star, Sawchuk had treated Leaf fans to a classic display of netminding.

He came off a bad outing in game four, when he was taunted by the Gardens crowd. One irate Leaf fan sent him a telegram: "How much did you get to throw the game?"

Sawchuk vowed to make the fan eat his words.

Rumours circulated that Sawchuk was in no condition to play, that he'd been drinking heavily the day before the game. Perhaps he'd played with a hangover. Who will ever know? "What a game he played tonight," praised his coach Punch Imlach. "Sawchuk never looked better than he did tonight. A lot of wise guys said we were too old, too beat up, that we couldn't beat Chicago in the semis or Montreal in the finals. Well, we shoved it right down their throats. Bower and Sawchuk, both older than dirt, were tremendous. And Sawchuk sure as hell ruined Montreal's plans to display the Stanley Cup at Expo 67."

● **In 1969–70,** at age 40, goalie Terry Sawchuk played his final season in New York. As a Ranger, he recorded his 103rd career shutout—an NHL record that stood for more than four decades. Martin Brodeur eclipsed the mark in 2010.

Following the 1969–70 season, Sawchuk and Ranger teammate Ron Stewart became involved in an unfortunate, alcohol-induced shoving match late one night. Sawchuk fell and injured himself badly, suffering a lacerated liver. Later, blood clots had to be removed, but one stopped his heart on May 31, 1970. Stewart was cleared of any responsibility for the incident.

Sawchuk was elected posthumously to the Hockey Hall of Fame in 1971 and was awarded the Lester Patrick Trophy for his contributions to hockey in the United States.

● **Goaltender Gerry Cheevers** of the Boston Bruins, one of the best of his era, was a member of both the 1970 and 1972 Stanley Cup–winning teams. In 1972, he went undefeated in 33 consecutive games, a record that stands to this day.

But it was his unusual mask that earned him a lot of attention. After a puck hit him in the face during practice one day, Cheevers went to the Boston dressing room to puff on a cigarette. While he was relaxing, John Forestall, the team trainer, painted stitch marks on his mask. After that, any time he was struck on the mask, new stitch marks were added. The mask became one of the most talked about face guards in hockey. The original mask is now on the wall of his grandson's bedroom. Another version of the mask is on display in the Hockey Hall of Fame. In 2008, *The Hockey News* rated his mask the greatest ever with a wide margin. Cheevers received 221 of a possible 300 points, while second-place Gilles Gratton got 66.

● **Sometimes it takes** a rookie goaltender a long time to win his first game with a new team. Sometimes the first win never comes. After breaking in with Philadelphia, where he won nine games in 1972–73, Michel Belhumeur moved on to the woeful Washington Capitals. In 1974–75, the poor chap went all season without winning a single game. His record was 0–24–3. The following season, he was 0–5–1. And that was it. Belhumeur never did win a game for Washington, or for any other NHL team. He finished his career in the minors.

● **In April 1974**, Pittsburgh Penguins goaltender Andy Brown became the last NHL goaltender to play without a mask, in a 6–3 loss to the Atlanta Flames.

● **In 1977,** goalie Al Smith of the Buffalo Sabres, miffed when the starting assignment he anticipated was given to rookie Don Edwards, waited until the pregame national anthem was played, then waved to the crowd, skated to the dressing room, took off his gear, and went home. Smith later became a taxi driver in Toronto and wrote plays in his spare time. His first play drew 17 spectators on opening night in 1998.

● **On February 25, 1978,** the Montreal Canadiens counted on extending their 28-game winning streak at the Montreal Forum. That night they faced the New York Rangers, who started a rookie goalie from Sweden—Hardy Astrom. It looked like easy pickings for the powerful Habs. But Astrom stunned Montreal with his puckstopping and skated off with a 6–3 victory. It would be his best game ever. Later he played for coach Don Cherry in Colorado. Cherry berated him constantly and nicknamed him the "Swedish Sieve."

● **On October 9, 1978,** the Los Angeles Kings were delighted to obtain goaltender Ron Grahame in a deal with

Boston. But they had no idea how much they were giving up to land the netminder. The draft choice they turned over to the Bruins turned out to be Ray Bourque, one of the greatest defencemen ever to play in the NHL.

● **In 1979,** an eye injury suffered by the Philadelphia Flyers' Bernie Parent caused all goaltenders to consider changing the face masks they wore. A high stick slipped through the right eyehole in Parent's mask and caused loss of vision, forcing him to retire. Many goalies began switching from the fibreglass mask to the cage and helmet model.

● **In 1983,** Hartford Whalers goalie John Garrett made several splendid saves in the annual All-Star Game and appeared to be the winner of a new car that goes to the game's MVP. Then Wayne Gretzky scored four third-period goals—an All-Star first—and stole the car away from Garrett.

● **Goalie Billy Smith** of the New York Islanders was the first NHL goalie to be credited with scoring a goal. On November 28, 1979, during a game against the Colorado Rockies, the puck bounced off Smith's chest while a delayed penalty was being called. Colorado's Rob Ramage shot the rebound back to the point, but there was nobody there. The puck slid down the ice into the empty net and Smith, the last Islander to touch it, was credited with the goal.

● **Almost 10 years later,** in 1988, goalie Ron Hextall of the Philadelphia Flyers became the first goalie to score a legitimate goal in the NHL when he fired a long shot down the ice into the Boston Bruins' empty net. Hextall repeated the feat a year later in a playoff game against the Washington Capitals.

The Devils' Marty Brodeur is the only other NHL goalie to score a regular season goal and a playoff goal.

● **When goalie** John Tanner made his NHL debut with the Quebec Nordiques on March 31, 1990, he became the seventh netminder to play for the team that season.

● **When the Quebec Nordiques** faced the Boston Bruins at the Boston Garden on March 21, 1991, Quebec goalie Ron Tugnutt knew he was in for a busy evening. He'd be facing renowned shooters such as Cam Neely and Ray Bourque, and he expected a heavy workload. But he didn't expect to be worn to a frazzle.

The 155-pound Tugnutt was pelted at the rate of more than a shot a minute, most of them sizzlers. But time and

again, the nimble netminder denied the Bruins glorious opportunities. With the game knotted 3–3, Tugnutt put on a display of overtime goaltending that brought the Bruins faithful to their feet in a seldom seen tribute to a gallant opponent. With seconds left to play in the overtime frame, Tugnutt robbed both Bourque and Neely of near certain goals to salvage a tie and a single point for his team. When the final buzzer sounded, the young man had stopped 70 of 73 shots to earn the respect and admiration of everyone in the building. As the crowd stood and roared, Neely skated up to the exhausted Tugnutt and said, "Take a bow. It's you they're applauding."

Most of the fans assumed the 73 shots on Tugnutt had set a league record. Not so. The mark for most shots in a game is held by a former Chicago netminder, Sam LoPresti, who was bombarded by 83 Boston shots in a game played 50 years earlier, almost to the day. Incredibly, Lopresti almost stole a win for the Hawks that night, finally losing 3–2.

The patriotic Lopresti joined the U.S. Navy shortly afterward, saying, "It may be safer facing Nazi U-boats in the Atlantic than dodging hockey pucks in the NHL." Ironically, he had plenty of time to consider that sentiment when his ship was torpedoed and he managed to survive for 45 days adrift on a life raft.

● **Goalie Ken Dryden's** NHL career was brief—a little more than seven full seasons. But his stats are unparalleled. His regular season totals include a .790 winning percentage, a 2.24 goals-against average, and, most incredibly, losing only 57 of 397 total games while recording 46 shutouts. No other modern-day goaltender has ever come close to earning nearly as many shutouts as recording losing games. He won the Vezina Trophy five times for allowing the fewest goals and five times was selected as a First Team All-Star. In 1998, he was ranked number 25 on *The Hockey News'* list of the 100 greatest hockey players.

● **Goaltenders rarely** pick up points, but one who did was Tom Barrasso, who in 1983 was the first netminder to jump from a U.S. high school team to the NHL. Barrasso played with six different teams over 19 seasons and collected a record 48 points in his career.

● **Goalie Terry Sawchuk** played for 20 seasons and finished his career with 103 shutouts. Experts said his shutout record would last forever. But in the 2009–10 season, his 16th, Martin Brodeur of the New Jersey Devils surpassed his mark and finished the season with 110. Brodeur also broke another goaltending record during that season: He played in his 1,076th game. The previous record holder was Patrick Roy, who retired after appearing in 1,029 games. Brodeur also holds the record for career wins by a goalie with 602.

Marty told me once, "Pete, you're a nice little puck, and you're welcome to hang around my goal crease. But don't you dare ever enter my net." Gee, I wonder if he was kidding.

● **I made a list** of some of Marty's most famous records at the end of the 2009–10 regular season. It's mind-boggling!

- Most regular season wins: 602
- Most shutouts: 110
- Most shutouts, regular season, and playoffs combined: 133
- Most overtime wins: 45
- Most consecutive 30-win seasons: 12
- Most consecutive 35-win seasons: 11
- Most 40-win seasons: 8
- Youngest goalie to reach 300, 400, and 500 career wins
- Most games played by an NHL goaltender: 1,076
- Most total minutes played by an NHL goaltender: 63,461
- Only NHL goalie to score a game-winning goal
- One of two NHL goalies (with Ron Hextall) to score a goal in both the regular season and the playoffs

● **Goalie Patrick Roy,** nicknamed "Saint Patrick," split his NHL career between Montreal and Colorado, winning two Stanley Cup championships with each franchise. In 1986, as a 20-year-old, Roy became the youngest player ever to win the Conn Smythe Trophy for playoff MVP, and he's the only player in NHL history to win the Conn Smythe Trophy three times. He is also credited with introducing the butterfly style of goaltending to hockey.

⬤ **On December 2, 1995,** Patrick Roy was in goal for Montreal during the Habs' worst defeat in club history—an 11–1 loss to Detroit. He allowed nine goals on 26 shots, and the crowd began to jeer him every time he made a save. When coach Mario Tremblay finally pulled him in the second period, Roy stormed past his coach and angrily confronted team president Ronald Corey, who was sitting nearby. "This is my last game in Montreal," he stated. Later, he told the media Tremblay kept him in the net to humiliate him. Four days later, Roy and team captain Mike Keane were traded to Colorado for goalie Jocelyn Thibault and forwards Martin Rucinsky and Andrei Kovalenko. The trade was considered one of the most one-sided deals in NHL history. It was sad to see the Habs stumble along without Saint Patrick. And Roy won two more Stanley Cups in Colorado.

⬤ **Did you know** that Patrick Roy was superstitious? He never skated over the lines on the ice—he jumped over them—and he talked to his goal posts. But I know this for certain: Very few of them ever talked back!

⬤ **Even though** Martin Brodeur has broken many of his records, Roy was voted the most outstanding goalie in NHL history by a panel of 41 writers plus a poll of fans. Hmmm. That poll may now be outdated. A second vote would probably make Brodeur number one.

⬤ **During the 1995–96** overseas season, Tony Melia of the British Ice Hockey League made history. His clearing shot down the ice was deflected past rival goalie Chris Brant, making Melia the only goalie to score a goal with the opposing goalie in the net. How embarrassing is that?

⬤**Hall of Fame** goalie Johnny Bower, born Johnny Kiszkan and nicknamed the "China Wall," played for many years with the Cleveland Barons of the American Hockey League before getting his big league chance with the Toronto Maple Leafs. One night, Cleveland played Providence and the Providence goalie was injured. There was no backup goalie available, so the teams agreed that Bower would switch jerseys and play for Providence. Bower said, "I gave my Cleveland mates lots of room to score, but they kept hitting me or missing the net. Cleveland was lucky to win by a couple of goals. After

the game, the Providence owner slipped me $50 for helping him out. That was a lot of money back then."

● **When Johnny** finally made it to the NHL with the Leafs, he was in his 30s. Even so, he won four Stanley Cups and was inducted into the Hockey Hall of Fame in 1978. He was so excited over one Cup win that he threw his goal stick high in the air to celebrate—and forgot it was up there. The stick came down and hit him on the head, opening a gash that required stitches. I loved Johnny Bower and felt bad every time someone shot me into his net.

● **Do you know** that an NHL goaltender who plays with equipment that hasn't been approved by the league, or who tampers with equipment after it has been approved, is subject to a two-game suspension and his club will be fined $25,000?

● **All NHL goaltenders** use a stick with a curved blade. The last known goalie to use a straight-bladed stick was Bill Ranford, who won two Stanley Cups with the Edmonton Oilers and a Conn Smythe Trophy. Ranford retired in 2000.

● **The first recorded** instance of a professional goalie scoring a goal occurred on February 21, 1971, in the Central Hockey League. In a game between the Oklahoma City Blazers and the Kansas City Blues, the Blazers were trailing 2–1 and decided to pull their goaltender. Michel Plasse, the goaltender for Kansas City, then scored into an open net.

● **Damian Rhodes** and José Théodore are the only goalies in NHL history to score a goal in a game in which they also had a shutout. Evgeni Nabokov of the San Jose Sharks was the first Russian goaltender to score a goal and the first goaltender to score a power play goal.

In 1997, a junior goalie, Ryan Venturelli of the Muskoka Bears, scored two goals in a game against the Durham Huskies. Muskoka won 11–6.

● **For the first time** in decades, a goalie has been named captain of an NHL team. Roberto Luongo is the captain of the Vancouver Canucks, even though there is a league rule forbidding goalies from holding that title. Why? Because goalies would spend too much time skating back and forth to discuss disputed plays with game officials. So Luongo does not wear a "C" on his jersey and lets his assistant captains do all the arguing. But he's still the team skipper and will speak for his teammates when discussions with coaches and management are called for.

Getting an Early Start FOUR

Even though Gordie Howe played NHL hockey into his 50s and others, such as Johnny Bower and Chris Chelios, were still going strong in their mid-40s, hockey is a young man's game. It's so cool to see kids like Sidney Crosby and Steven Stamkos emerge from junior hockey and become instant stars in the NHL. I love to see the rookies keep pace with the vets, especially when they stay focused and don't let all the media attention and the big money go to their heads.

● **The youngest goalie** to play in a Stanley Cup playoff game was 17-year-old Albert Forrest. In 1905, he was the netminder on a team that travelled 4,000 miles to make a grab for Lord Stanley's Cup. Poor Albert. Playing for Yukon's Dawson City Nuggets against Ottawa's Silver Seven, he lost both games, one by a score of 23–2, a playoff record.

● **The youngest goalie** ever to play in the NHL was Harry "Apple Cheeks" Lumley. In 1942–43, when he was just 17 years old, Lumley was loaned by the Detroit Red Wings to the New York Rangers for a single game. In 1950, Lumley led Detroit to the Stanley Cup and recorded three playoff shutouts. His reward? Manager Jack Adams traded him to the Chicago Black Hawks.

● **Don "Bones" Raleigh** was one of the most popular players in New York Rangers history. He joined the club in 1943 at age 17 and remains the youngest player to have ever played for the team.

● **A teenager once owned** an NHL hockey club. When Major Fred McLaughlin, owner of the Chicago Black Hawks, died in 1944, he left his team to his 16-year-old son.

● **In March 1966,** 14-year-old Doug Bentley Jr. became the youngest player outside the NHL to take part in a professional hockey game. With permission from the league, Bentley played in a game between the Knoxville Knights and the Jacksonville Rockets.

● **Since 1950,** a player must be 18 years old to play for a team in the NHL. The youngest player in NHL history was Armand "Bep" Guidolin, who was only 16 when he joined the Boston Bruins in November 1942. Can you imagine the kidding he took from his teammates? Are you homesick, kid? Are you old enough to shave? Ever eaten in a fancy restaurant, kid?

Young Guidolin scored 7 goals and added 15 assists for 22 points as a rookie. He later played with Chicago and Detroit and coached in the NHL with Boston and Kansas City.

● **When Guy Lafleur** started out in hockey, he used to sleep in his equipment. That way, he was ready to play in the morning.

He would often start playing at 7 or 8 a.m., then play again at noon and again after school until it got dark.

At the International Pee Wee Hockey Tournament in Quebec City in 1962, Lafleur emerged as the outstanding player of the tournament. On his 15th birthday, weighing just 135 pounds, Guy joined the ranks of junior A players in Quebec. In 1970–71, Guy scored an unprecedented 130 goals and 209 points, both Quebec Junior Hockey League bests, and was named to the league's First All-Star team. He then followed with 22 goals, 21 assists, and 43 points in the 1971 playoffs to lead all point producers during the post-season. That spring, with Lafleur leading the way, the Remparts won the Memorial Cup.

● **Wayne Cashman** was the zaniest if not the meanest and toughest member of the big bad Boston Bruins of the seventies. "I knew I'd never be a 50-goal scorer, so I spent my career doing what had to be done," Cashman told *Sports Illustrated* while toiling in the twilight of his career.

As a young boy, Wayne Cashman couldn't wait to play hockey. One day, on the family farm near Kingston, Ontario, where he grew up, he acquired a new pair of skates. Told by his parents not to wear them outside because of below-zero temperatures, Cashman waited until his parents went off somewhere. Then he opened all the windows, hooked up a hose, and flooded the kitchen floor with an inch of water. When it freezes, he reasoned, I'll skate inside.

When his parents returned earlier than expected, well, you can guess the rest of the story.

● **Wayne Gretzky** has set more scoring records than any player in NHL history. He started early, playing with 10-year-olds when he was only six. At age 11, he scored 378 goals in 85 games, and by the time he was a teenager, he'd scored 1,000 goals. In the early 1970s, he was getting as much attention from the media as some professionals. At the 15th annual International Pee Wee Hockey Tournament in Quebec City, 13,000 fans tried to get into a 10,000-seat arena to marvel at the only pee wee player to score 378 goals in a season. In four games, Gretzky scored 13 goals and added 13 assists for his Brantford club. In a game against Texas, Brantford won 25–0.

Every season, the sweater he was given would be far too large for Wayne. He coped by tucking the sweater into his pants on the right side. He continued doing this throughout his NHL career.

● **Only two** 17-year-olds have been selected number one in the NHL's annual Entry Draft: Buffalo's Pierre Turgeon (1987) and Boston's Joe Thornton (1997).

⬤ **During the 2003–04** season, 12-year-old John Tavares scored 95 goals and 187 points in 90 games and led the Toronto Marlboros bantam team to the 2004 Bantam AAA Provincial Hockey Championships. The Marlboros defeated the London Junior Knights 5–0 in the championship game and Tavares was named the tournament's top forward. The following season, he joined the Marlboros' minor midget team, where he recorded 91 goals and 158 points in 72 games. During this season, age 13, he also played 16 games with the Milton Icehawks of the Ontario Provincial Junior A Hockey League, during which he recorded 11 goals and 23 points. People couldn't recall when someone so young had played junior hockey. In 2005, the Ontario Hockey League introduced an "exceptional player" clause that allowed young phenoms to play in the league. Tavares was drafted by the Oshawa Generals and at age 14 became the youngest player drafted into the OHL. (Bobby Orr had played with Oshawa as a 14-year-old, but he hadn't been drafted.) At age 15, during his rookie season, Tavares scored 45 goals and 77 points and was named the Canadian Hockey League's rookie of the year.

⬤ **Sidney Crosby** was only two and a half years old when his father began teaching him the fundamentals of hockey. They played on the floor of the basement in the Crosby home in Cole Harbour, Nova Scotia. Crosby often practised shooting the puck at the opening of the family's clothes dryer. Lots of black marks on that machine, I'll bet. I wonder what his parents thought when they found hockey pucks mixed in with the laundry. Incidentally, my pals in Pittsburgh tell me Crosby is the most dedicated, clean-living hockey player they've ever seen. Off the ice, his drink of choice is not beer or cola—but milk! In 2007, Crosby's milk drinking paid off. At the age of 19 years and 244 days, he won the NHL scoring championship with 120 points, the youngest Art Ross Trophy winner in history.

In 2010, Sidney scored one of the most famous goals in hockey history. His overtime marker in the gold medal game at the Vancouver Olympics gave Canada a hard-fought victory over a gallant U.S. team.

● **Minnesota's high school** hockey tournament is the largest state sports tournament in the United States in terms of attendance. It attracts more fans than either the Florida and Texas state high school football tournaments or the Indiana state basketball tournament. Attendance at the 2008 Minnesota championship tourney surpassed 100,000, with some games drawing 18,000 spectators.

● **Daniel and Henrik Sedin,** the twin brothers who star for the Vancouver Canucks, attended high school in Sweden while playing professionally for the Modo Hockey club. They were only 16 years old. In their second year with Modo, Daniel led a team that included future NHLers Samuel Påhlsson and František Kaberle in scoring with 42 points in 50 games. Henrik finished tied for second. Daniel and Henrik were then named co-recipients of the Golden Puck as Swedish players of the year.

Henrik and Daniel both entered the 1999 draft with the expectation of being selected separately. However, after some clever dealing, Vancouver Canucks general manager Brian Burke obtained the second and third overall picks in order to select both Daniel and Henrik. In 2009, they agreed to identical five-year, $30.5-million contracts.

Early in the 2009–10 season, Daniel suffered a broken foot after taking a slapshot from a teammate. During the last game of the season, on April 10, 2010, Daniel scored his fourth career NHL hat trick in a 7–3 win against the Calgary Flames. All three goals were assisted by his brother, helping Henrik pass Alexander Ovechkin for the Art Ross Trophy.

● **Today, the annual** NHL Entry Draft is a nationally televised showcase event. It's hard to believe that the NHL's post-season Entry Draft was once conducted in secret—with all the choices being made over the telephone!

In 1974, the hush-hush draft was held behind closed doors because the NHL clubs feared growing competition for young players by a new pro league, the upstart World Hockey Association. The telephone draft spanned three days. The Buffalo Sabres contributed the most shocking—and most amusing—twist. General manager Punch Imlach selected a little-known Japanese star, Taro Tsujimoto, in the 11th round. Taro? Who's Taro? Imlach described Tsujimoto as "a 5' 8", 180-pound playmaker from the Tokyo Katanas." NHL scouts and coaches scratched their heads. Nobody had heard of this Taro chap. Or the Tokyo Katanas. He would have been the first Asian player to be drafted.

Over the next few days, Buffalo reporters hounded Imlach, demanding to know more about Tsujimoto. "Wait'll you see this guy in training camp," Imlach answered. "He'll really surprise you with his skills."

But Tsujimoto didn't show up for training camp.

Only then did Imlach confess his selection of the Japanese star had been a practical joke. He'd plucked Tsujimoto's name from the Buffalo telephone book. No such hockey player existed.

But the hoax didn't die. Years later, Buffalo fans were still flashing "WE WANT TARO" signs at Sabres games.

● **Have you noticed** how long it's been since a rookie with the Montreal Canadiens has won the Calder Trophy? It's been almost 30 years since goalie Ken Dryden edged Richard Martin of the Buffalo Sabres, a 44-goal scorer, for the coveted Calder in 1972. Montreal's Guy Lafleur wasn't even close in the balloting that season.

Jacques Lemaire came close in 1968, only to be edged by Derek Sanderson of the Bruins. Two Habs vied for the trophy in 1964, with Jacques Laperriere nosing out John Ferguson. Phil Esposito was eligible that season but scored a mere 3 goals in 27 games for Chicago. Bobby Rousseau won it in 1962 (over Boston's Cliff Pennington, who scored a grand total of 17 goals in more than 100 games), Ralph Backstrom in 1959 (over the Leafs' Carl Brewer), and Bernie Geoffrion in 1952 (over Hy Buller of New York).

The first Hab to win the Calder was Johnny Quilty in 1941. Quilty scored 18 goals and 34 points in his freshman season. He never matched those totals, and within three years he was gone from the NHL.

Rocket Richard made his debut in 1942–43 but broke his ankle after 16 games. The Leafs' Gaye Stewart skated off with the award and Montreal's Glen Harmon was runner-up.

The Rocket was still eligible the following season. He scored 32 goals in 46 games and no doubt fumed when Toronto's Gus Bodnar captured the Calder with 22 goals in 50 games. To be fair, Bodnar outpointed Richard 62–54.

Jean Beliveau was favoured to win the Calder in 1954 but played in only 44 games, scored 13 goals, and finished behind winner Camille Henry of New York and Earl Reibel of Detroit.

The Calder drought began after Dryden's win in 1972. The Habs' Chris Chelios came close in 1985, if finishing second to Mario Lemieux can be called close.

● **Several of the NHL's** greatest stars failed to win the Calder Trophy. Habs defenceman Doug Harvey won seven Norris Trophies in eight seasons for Montreal but didn't get a nod for the rookie award in 1948 (Detroit's Jim McFadden was the winner). Gordie Howe finished behind both Howie Meeker of the Leafs and Jim Conacher of Detroit in 1947. And Wayne Gretzky, despite registering 51 goals and 137 points in his first NHL season (1979–80), was ruled ineligible for Calder consideration. The previous season, as an 18-year-old, he'd scored 110 points in the WHA, making him "too experienced" to be considered an NHL rookie. Quebec's Peter Stastny was the 1980 winner.

● **Brit Selby** of the Toronto Maple Leafs was the Calder Trophy winner in 1965–66. He may have been the weakest choice for the rookie award in history. His total of 27 points is the lowest scoring total by a Calder-winning forward since 1938, when seasons were 48 games long. Selby held a points-per-game average of 0.337 in his freshman season, which stands as the lowest points-per-game average of any non-goalie Calder winner in history.

Women Love Hockey, Too **FIVE**

Canadian men may have been first on the ice, first to carve a stick from a bent tree limb, and first to smack a flat piece of wood or a rubber ball or, ahem, a frozen horse ball around an ice-covered pond or creek. But women were close behind. They, too, wanted to experience the joy of playing shinny with their brothers and their friends. And they were welcome. Games need bodies, and sisters and girlfriends were often recruited to fill out a couple of teams. I'm sure even a few grandmas were persuaded to play in goal from time to time.

It wasn't long before women were forming their own teams. And my, how some of them could play! But there was often a problem.

Many girls learned to play wearing figure skates, but picks in the blade tripped them up. A player was forced to take shorter strides if hockey was her game. So girls got their mittened hands on hockey skates, often their brothers' hand-me-downs. Failing that, they had the picks ground off. What a difference it made!

● **As early as 1890,** women wearing long skirts, bulky sweaters, and stocking caps were playing organized women's hockey games. Lord Stanley's daughter Isobel (who later became Lady Isobel Gathorne-Hardy) and her friends played on the outdoor ice next to Government House in Ottawa. In 1899, a game was arranged between the Government House team and the Rideau ladies, conceivably the first women's hockey game in history. Lady Isobel wore a long white dress when she played. If high society ladies like the refined Lady Isobel and her cultured friends could enjoy the pleasures of hockey, why couldn't any woman with a pair of skates and a stick try her hand at the game? And thousands did.

⬤ **Some women** crouched down in front of their goalie. Their long skirts would spread out on the ice, and the material stopped a lot of shots from going in the goal.

● **Women enrolled** at McGill University in Montreal began playing organized games on an indoor rink as early as 1894. They were granted four hours of ice time per week, provided three supervisors were on duty to guard the entrances. No male students were allowed in. And no photographers. The referee blew his whistle three times—to start the game, to signal half-time, and to end the contest.

● **Women in Stratford,** Ontario, had begun to play the game in a new arena in town by 1895. Men were strictly forbidden from entering the arena when women were at play. The players' names were never published, and no photographs of them were ever taken.

● **In 1899,** Lady Minto, wife of Canada's Governor General, Lord Minto, took part in hockey games played at the Rideau Skating Rink in Ottawa. A reporter wrote: "The ladies played with vim quite foreign to their natures. And the manner in which Lady Minto went up the ice was a revelation to the other players. Some time earlier, Lady Minto broke her leg while skating."

● **American women** began to show an interest in hockey in the late 1800s. In 1899, two women's teams faced off at the Philadelphia Ice Palace, where they played on artificial ice.

● **In the early 1900s,** women wore homemade chest pads stitched together out of unbleached cotton. The pads had long pockets stuffed with sawdust, available from most backyards or workshops at the time, till they were an inch or two thick. The flap was closed and sewn tight to prevent the sawdust from spilling out.

● **In 1900,** the first known league for women was organized in Quebec with three teams competing and male spectators, at long last, allowed to attend. Western Canadian women were keeping pace with their eastern counterparts. Teams with colourful names sprang up: the Biggar Floradoras, the Saskatchewan Prairie Lilies, the Snowflakes, the Golden Girls, and even a team called the Old Hens.

● **Early newspaper** reports indicate that bodychecking in women's hockey was frowned upon. In 1905, a reporter wrote: "Miss Janet Allen was ruled off the ice for one minute for being a bad girl. She checked one of the Richview girls real hard."

● **The first female** hockey star to attract national attention was Cornwall, Ontario's Albertine Lapensée. Playing for her hometown Vics during World War I, Lapensée drew huge crowds to the arenas she played in. It's said she scored 80 per cent of her team's goals. Her shot was so powerful that an opposing goalie scrambled, at least in one game, to find a catcher's mask to protect her face—a full decade before goalie Elizabeth Graham would be credited with introducing the face mask to hockey when she donned a fencing mask at Queen's University. After two sensational seasons, Lapensée disappeared. Her nephew said she went to New York and reappeared weeks later—as a man! She had changed her name to Albert Smyth and never played hockey again.

● **Thora Mills,** a Toronto player on a 1924–25 championship team, once described her equipment: "We had arm and leg pads and, as the goalie, I wore a chest protector. That was about it. We had no dressing rooms, no showers, no face masks and no indoor ice. We played outdoors almost all the time. And we were modest, undressing in front of each other very discreetly. We never stood up naked in front of the team. And we always travelled with a chaperone."

⬤ **Many years ago,** the University of Toronto women's hockey team had many fine players but no goalie. The women solved their problem by approaching the biggest woman on campus and recruiting her to fill the position. The young woman was willing, but there was a problem—she had no idea how to skate.

"We'll teach you," promised the other players. But it wasn't an easy task. Finding skates large enough for their new recruit proved difficult. And fitting her into them took time and energy. Before each game, her teammates helped her into her equipment and then propelled her across the ice and propped her up between the goal posts.

"Promise me I won't have to stop a lot of pucks," she pleaded.

"We promise."

And they kept their word. In one game, the awkward novice made three stops. In two other games, she made two stops in each. In another game, she turned aside one puck, and in the remaining two games, she made no stops at all— no pucks were directed her way.

Her goal posts became her friends and she hugged them tenaciously. Every time she released one of them, she collapsed in a heap. Her teammates spent most of each intermission getting her on and off the ice. It was hard work but well worth it. By the end of the season, she'd earned a sparkling goals-against average and was proud to accept her crest as a member of the championship team. "Hockey can't get any better than this for me," she announced after the final game. "So I think I'll quit while I'm ahead."

● **Hilda Ranscombe** starred with the Preston, Ontario, Rivulettes throughout the 1930s. A dazzling skater, Ranscombe led her team to six Dominion Championships. One statistician lists their record at 345–2–3. And, as is typical with hockey players, there was trash talking and fighting.

Incidentally, those two losses took place in Edmonton after a gruelling train ride and with most of the Preston players battling the flu. Edmonton won by scores of 2–1 and 1–0. Illness forced the Rivulettes to play shorthanded in the second game.

● **Fran Westman,** a University of Toronto star in the early 1930s, formed a team called the Vagabonds upon graduation. For a 1933 game in Port Dover, posters advertised Westman as the "outstanding lady hockeyist in Ontario." Did she excel in the contest? No. She was newly married, and her husband refused to let her play. "She had another game to play the following day," he explained, "and two games in two days is too much for a woman—in my opinion." I'll bet that Fran, if she was playing today, would tell her husband to take a hike and go to both games.

● **During World War II,** women shifted their priorities. They focused on family matters and the work force while men served in the armed forces. Women's hockey declined and did not make a comeback until the 1960s.

● **In 1955,** eight-year-old Abby Hoffman cut off most of her hair and signed on as Ab Hoffman in the Toronto hockey league. She became the first female player to create a sensation by starring in an all-boys league. Hoffman's gender was kept secret until the playoffs, when birth certificates were checked. She was allowed to continue playing and was in-vited to Maple Leaf Gardens to be a guest on *Hockey Night in Canada*. She went on to become an Olympic athlete—but in track, not in hockey. In 1972, she captured a bronze medal in the 800-metre race in Munich, Germany.

● **By 1982,** a national championship for women had been reintroduced and a female hockey council was established. In 1987, the first Women's World Hockey Tournament was held in North York, Ontario—a tournament that spawned other major championships in Europe and Asia.

● **Samantha Holmes** was eight years old when she trav-elled with her family to watch hockey games at the 1988 Winter Olympic Games in Calgary, Alberta. She was sur-prised and disappointed when she was told that women's hockey was not an Olympic sport. Weeks later, she wrote a letter to Prime Minister Brian Mulroney and her home-town mayor, Hazel McCallion, in Mississauga, Ontario, asking that they help get women's hockey into the Olympics. Holmes's persistent efforts were rewarded when women's hockey was debuted as a medal sport at the 1998 Olympic Winter Games in Nagano, Japan.

● **Holmes was smart** to appeal to Hazel McCallion. The long-time Mississauga mayor was one of the first females to "play for pay." She moved from a small town in the Gaspe to Montreal during the early 1940s and was recruited to play in a women's league—for $5 a game. McCallion has been a great booster of Canadian women's hockey and still dons the blades occasionally. She'll be 90 years old on Valentine's Day, 2011. You're a hockey heroine, Hazel.

⬤ **On June 22, 1988,** a Windsor area woman became the first hockey player to be convicted of assaulting an official during a game. In 1986, nurse Trudy Banwell, then 24, was playing for a women's team from Harrow in the provincial championships in Mississauga when she slammed referee Angela James to the ice. Then she assaulted linesman Barb Jeffrey, separating her shoulder. Convicted of two counts of assault, Banwell was given a conditional discharge and two years' probation, and ordered to serve 200 hours of community service. The Ontario Women's Hockey Association handed Banwell a lifetime suspension.

⬤ **The first** Women's World Hockey Championships were held in Ottawa in 1990. Team Canada wore pink uniforms and captured the title with a victory over the United States. A 16-year-old Ottawa girl sang the national anthem. Before the game, I asked her, "What's your name, miss?" And she said, "Alanis Morissette." She went on to a great career in pop music. Wish I'd thought to get her autograph.

⬤ **The Winter Olympics** of 1998 provided a global stage for women players. At Nagano, Japan, Team USA upset Canada to win the first Olympic gold medal. Four years later, at Salt Lake City, after compiling an impressive 31–0–0 record in pre-Olympic play, the defending champions were upset by Canada by a 3–2 score. Team Canada had to overcome 11 U.S. power play opportunities, including 11 in a row, en route to their most memorable triumph ever.

⬤ **Canada's Manon Rhéaume** became the first female goalie to play in an NHL preseason game, with the Tampa Bay Lightning. While she never played in a regular season game, she did perform well in the minor pro leagues and with Canada's national women's team. She led Canada to world championships in 1992 and 1994 and captured a silver medal at the 1998 Olympics.

⬤ **On October 30, 1993,** American Erin Whitten became the first female goalie to win a professional game, in the East Coast Hockey League, when the Toledo Storm edged the Dayton Bombers 6–5. She did not play in the entire game. In 1995–96, she would become the first woman to play and win an entire regular season professional hockey game. She accomplished this feat with the Flint Generals in a 6–5 victory over the Detroit Falcons. While with Flint, she also became the first woman to play as a forward in a pro game. Because of injuries and suspensions, she played 18 seconds and served a bench penalty for the Generals. Whitten was also the first woman to play a game in the American Hockey League. During the 1993–94 preseason, she played for the Adirondack Red Wings.

⬤ **In 2003,** Canadian superstar Hayley Wickenheiser, playing for HC Salamat of the Finnish National League, became the first woman to score a goal in a men's professional league. In 2010, Hayley became the leading female hockey goal scorer in Olympic history. I predict you'll see her in the Hockey Hall of Fame soon after she retires.

⬤ **Is it possible** to score 82 goals in a 60-minute hockey game? Obviously it is, because in 2008 the Slovakian women's team whitewashed Bulgaria 82–0. It was a record score for an IIHF-sanctioned women's event. Slovakia, which won all four of its games at the tournament in Latvia, outshot Bulgaria 139–0, scoring on 58.9 percent of its shots on goal. Slovakia averaged one goal every 44 seconds.

The drubbing capped a woeful showing for the Bulgarian women, who had also lost 30–1 to Croatia and 41–0 to Italy in earlier games.

● **Mickey Walker** of Bala, Ontario, who passed away at age 90 in 2009, was the oldest Canadian Amateur Hockey Associated–registered female player in the world. She continued to play the game at least once a week well into her 80s.

● **Kathryn Waldo** is a legend at Northeastern University in Boston, where she studied from 1995 through 1999. She led the Huskies in scoring with 15 goals as a freshman and by her senior season had also earned the Eastern College Athletic Conference Award of Valor. In 1997, she inspired her team to the ECAC division 1 championship. She scored 52 goals and 106 points in her college career—19th best in the school's history.

And she did it all while battling cystic fibrosis. Though she had it since she was a little girl, she never let the disease stop her.

● **Cassie Campbell** is one of the most famous female hockey players in the world. Campbell is the only Canadian hockey player, male or female, to captain a national team to two Olympic gold medals, winning in 2002 in Salt Lake City and 2006 in Turin. The team also won an Olympic silver medal in Nagano in 1998. During her career, Campbell captured six world titles and won a total of 21 international tournament medals—17 gold and four silver.

The 1.7-metre (5 foot, 7 inches), 68-kilogram (150 pounds) player joined the national team in 1994 as a defenceman but became a forward in 1998. She retired with 32 goals and 68 assists in 157 career games.

● **On February 25, 2010,** Canada's women's hockey team defeated the United States 2–0 to capture the gold medal at the 2010 Winter Olympics in Vancouver. Goalie Shannon Szabados made 28 saves en route to her shutout, and Meghan Agosta was voted tournament MVP for her nine-goal performance—an Olympic record.

The Canadian team celebrated the win by smoking cigars and drinking beer at centre ice—after the arena emptied—which upset some people. They apologized, and that ended the matter.

● **The twin sisters** Jocelyne and Monique Lamoureux played on the U.S. Olympic team in 2010. Hockey is a family tradition in the Lamoureux home. The women, from Grand Forks, North Dakota, have four older brothers who play the sport and would mix it up with them in pickup games. Jean-Philippe, 25, is a goalie in the Buffalo Sabres system; Jacques, 23, an Air Force Academy forward; Pierre-Paul, 22, a University of North Dakota student volunteer assistant coach; and Mario, 21, a U of North Dakota forward. Their dad, Pierre, a backup goalie, played on the University of North Dakota's national championship teams of 1980 and 1982. No wonder the sisters are Olympians.

● **Do you know** that 12 women have had their names engraved on the Stanley Cup? The first woman to have her name engraved on the Stanley Cup is Marguerite Norris, who was president of the Detroit Red Wings in 1954 and 1955. The only Canadian woman to have her name engraved on the Cup is Sonia Scurfield (born in Hafford, Saskatchewan), who won the Cup as a co-owner of the Calgary Flames in 1989.

The Colorado Avalanche's senior director of hockey

administration, Charlotte Grahame, had her name added when the Avalanche won in 2001. Charlotte's son, John, later had his name engraved as a goaltender on the Tampa Bay Lightning, making them the only mother-son combination to win the Stanley Cup.

Stanley Cup Facts and Follies SIX

⬤ **The Stanley Cup** was a gift to Canadian hockey from Lord Stanley of Preston, an English nobleman who was Governor General from 1888 to 1893. Ironically, Lord Stanley never saw a Stanley Cup game and never got to present the trophy, which at that time was a small silver bowl he'd purchased for less than $50. He was recalled to England before the first Cup game was played. Few can recall if he gave any other gifts to Canada before he departed. It doesn't matter. Leaving us the Stanley Cup was more than enough. It means we'll always remember him fondly.

⬤ **Originally,** the Stanley Cup was a challenge trophy. Several teams from various leagues competed for it. My favourite Stanley Cup challenge story involved a team of gold miners from the Yukon. Starting out on December 19, 1904, the Dawson City Nuggets travelled 4,000 miles—by foot, bicycle, dog sled, ship, and train—to get to Ottawa. Early in 1905, they played a much superior team, the Ottawa Silver Seven. Exhausted from their long journey, and with no chance to practise en route, the Nuggets were walloped 9–2 and 23–2 in a best-of-three series. It was the most lopsided series in Stanley Cup history.

● **Did you know** there are three Stanley Cups? The original silver bowl is about the size of a football: 18.5 centimetres (7.28 inches) in height and 29 centimetres (11.42 inches) in diameter. It is always on display at the Hockey Hall of Fame in Toronto. The current Stanley Cup—the authenticated one—is made of silver and nickel alloy. It was created in 1963 by Montreal silversmith Carl Petersen. The third Cup is a clone of the authentic Cup and is used as a stand in from time to time for the authentic Cup. The authentic Cup is the one you see at playoff time, It is 89.54 centimetres (35.25 inches) high and weighs 15.5 kilograms (34.5 pounds). You've seen players throw it over their heads when they win it. I tried to lift it one year and it wouldn't budge.

● **In 1994,** Carl Petersen's son Ole was not amused when he learned that New York Ranger forward Ed Olczyk was photographed using the Cup to feed oats to Kentucky Derby winner Go for Gin at Belmont Park one afternoon. "It's unpardonable," snorted Ole Petersen. "Imagine treating the Cup with such little respect. My father must be spinning in his grave."

Olczyk quickly explained that the photo was a publicity shot and that the horse didn't actually dine from the Cup. "It just looked that way. There were no oats in the bowl."

● **It's traditional** for players on the winning team to drink champagne from the Stanley Cup. Just for fun, after the Penguins won it in 2009, one of the Pittsburgh players dunked me in the bowl of the Cup and I had to swim for my life. And boy, did I have the hiccups!

⬤ **Some players** have taken the Cup to bed with them. Others have fed their dog from it, and some of the curious ones have taken it apart to see what's inside. In 1924, the Cup was left on a street corner in Montreal when some celebrating players stopped to change a flat tire. After the turn of the last century, on a dare, the Cup was tossed into the Rideau Canal in Ottawa, but luckily the canal was frozen and the Cup recovered. After the Leafs won it in 1964, Hall of Famer Red Kelly's infant son was plunked in the Cup for a photo, and guess what he did? I won't say, but it was fortunate that he had on his diaper.

● **The Stanley Cup** differs from other major sport trophies in that the names of winning players, coaches, and managers are engraved on its surface. Over the years, a lot of names have been misspelled. And each member of the winning organization gets to keep it for a day in the off-season. It's the oldest and most famous team trophy there is.

● **The first U.S. city** to capture the Stanley Cup was Seattle, Washington, a PCHA team. In 1916–17, the Seattle Metropolitans beat the Montreal Canadiens by three games to one in the final series. The Cup engraver misspelled Canadiens as "Canadians" after the series.

● **After the** New York Rangers won the Stanley Cup in 1940, defeating Toronto in the finals, the Rangers celebrated back at their hotel—the Royal York. They drank some beer from Lord Stanley's big basin and smoked cigars. The next day, half the team boarded a train for New York while others headed off to western Canada. New Yorkers were pleased with the triumph, but there was no big celebration. Nobody considered holding a victory parade or ordering championship rings. The players were given gold watches worth about $30. Stanley Cup rings would come 50 years later.

● **In 1990,** Rangers general manager Neil Smith decided that the seven surviving members of the 1940 championship squad had waited long enough. He presented each of them with an expensive Stanley Cup ring to mark the golden anniversary of a memorable moment in Rangers history.

● **On April 12, 1941,** the Boston Bruins established a new Stanley Cup record with an easy victory over Detroit in the Cup finals. The Bruins won in four straight games, an unprecedented accomplishment. And they did it without the services of Bill Cowley, their star player, the league's leading scorer and most valuable player in 1940–41. Cowley suffered a knee injury during the playoffs and took part in only two games in the semifinals.

In the finals against Detroit, after the Red Wings had suffered through three consecutive losses by scores of 3–2, 2–1 and 4–2, Red Wings fans showed little support for their team during game four at the Olympia, won by the Bruins 4–1. Only 8,125 showed up—half as many as witnessed the first two games at the Boston Garden.

There was a brief presentation at centre ice following the game. Handshakes were exchanged, and then the champions headed for the railroad station, where they caught the train back to Boston.

● **Hector "Toe" Blake** often said that his personal high as a playoff performer took place in the 1944 playoffs when he sparked Montreal to a 5–4 overtime victory over Chicago in the fourth and final game of the Stanley Cup finals. The Habs were trailing by three goals in the final period of game four when Blake assisted on three straight Montreal goals that made it a tie. Then, after nine minutes of overtime, he slapped in the game winner as 12,880 fans roared their appreciation. Blake's five-point night gave him a new playoff points record of 18, and the win climaxed Montreal's most successful season ever. Aside from winning eight straight playoff games over Toronto and Chicago, they set a new regular season scoring mark of 234 goals and a regular season point record of 83. Not big numbers by today's standards but impressive back then.

● **The Montreal Canadiens** are the only NHL team to win the Stanley Cup five times in a row. They dominated the playoffs from 1956 through 1960. Jean Béliveau, one of my favourite players, starred on those teams.

● **At least once,** a rabid fan tried to prevent the Stanley Cup from being presented to a rival team. During a 1962 playoff game in Chicago, Ken Kilander, a Montrealer, watched his beloved Canadiens fail to stop the surging Black Hawks. Kilander bolted from his seat, ran to the lobby of Chicago Stadium, and smashed open a glass case holding the Cup. He darted away with the trophy, only to be chased and arrested by police. In court the following morning, he

told the judge, "I was just taking it back to Montreal where it belongs." The judge said, "You go back to Montreal. The Stanley Cup stays here."

● **In the spring** of 1944, Maurice "Rocket" Richard of the Montreal Canadiens put on one of the greatest offensive displays in Stanley Cup history. The Canadiens played the Toronto Maple Leafs in a semifinal series that year. Big Bob Davidson, a tenacious checker, was closely shadowing Richard, a second-year man who'd scored 32 goals during the regular season. After his Canadiens lost by a 3–1 score in the opener, Richard predicted a different outcome in game two.

Two minutes into the second period, Richard raced in to beat Paul Bibeault for the game's first goal. Seventeen

seconds later, he came back and scored again. Toronto fought back with a goal, but before the buzzer Richard scored again. It was his third goal of the period—a Stanley Cup hat trick.

In the third period, the Rocket stayed hot and scored two more goals. Final score: Richard 5, Toronto 1. The last time a player had scored five or more goals in a playoff game had been back in 1917. Fans threw hats and programs in the air when it was announced that Richard had earned all three stars for his performance. It's the only time an NHL player has been saluted in such a manner.

● **The Boston Bruins** iced fabulous teams in 1970 and 1972 when they skated off with two Stanley Cups. A remarkable photo of Bobby Orr flying through the air in front of St. Louis Blues goalie Glenn Hall is one of the greatest hockey photos of the century. Orr's overtime goal was the Cup winner in 1970. Phil Esposito remembers waking up on his front lawn early the next morning with the Stanley Cup in his arms.

At the time, 1970, Orr's 120 points during the regular season were more than twice as many as any other defence-man had scored in one season in the entire history of the NHL. One year later, he was even more productive, garnering 139 points. The Oilers' Paul Coffey threatened Orr's 139 point mark in 1985–86 but fell 1 point shy, finishing with 138 points.

Add Boston's Ray Bourque to the list with his career points record of 1,579, ahead of Coffey and Orr, and these three fellows reign as the most prolific defencemen in the history of hockey.

⬤ **When the Montreal Canadiens** opened the 1971 playoffs, they were given little chance against the powerful Boston Bruins, led by superstars Bobby Orr and Phil Esposito. The Bruins had won 15 more games than the Canadiens and finished with 24 more points.

The Bruins were stunned to see Ken Dryden—a raw rookie—start in goal for Montreal. Had coach Al MacNeil lost his mind? They'd show this rookie netminder what playoff pressure was all about. As expected, Boston took the opening game 3–1, and in game two, the Bruins waltzed off to a 5–1 lead.

Suddenly the Canadiens began to fight back. They scored a goal, then another, then four more to take a 7–5 lead. The Bruins were obviously rattled by the second period barrage, but they weren't about to concede. They launched a third period assault on Dryden.

But the lanky goaltender turned aside shot after shot. Some of his saves were truly magnificent. And when the final buzzer sounded, he'd won his first playoff game.

In game two, Dryden continued to give Montreal spectacular goaltending and the Canadiens eventually eliminated the frustrated Bruins in seven games.

The Canadiens went on to defeat the Chicago Black Hawks in the final series for the Stanley Cup. Once again, Dryden played a key role in the victory. At season's end, he was awarded the Conn Smythe Trophy as MVP of the playoffs, a remarkable achievement for an inexperienced newcomer.

The following season, he continued to play brilliantly and skated off with the Calder Trophy as the league's top freshman. No player in history had been a playoff MVP one season and a rookie award winner the next.

Dryden went on to win 258 games for Montreal while

losing only 57. His .758 winning percentage is the best goaltending average in NHL history. He helped the Habs to win six Stanley Cups and was inducted into the Hockey Hall of Fame in 1983.

⬤**After the Boston Bruins** won the Stanley Cup in 1970 over the Blues on Bobby Orr's sensational "flying high in the air" goal in overtime, Orr sought a familiar face in the crowd. Then he escorted defenceman Ted Green onto the ice. Green, Boston's toughest defenceman, had been severely injured in a preseason game, a stick-swinging duel with the Blues' Wayne Maki that left Green partially paralyzed. He didn't suit up for a single game and feared his career might be over. When Green saluted the roaring crowd at Bobby's side, all the Bruins and all the fans had tears in their eyes. Green eventually returned to hockey and played several more seasons. He won a second Stanley Cup with Boston in 1972 and five more in a coaching role with the Edmonton Oilers in the eighties.

In 1972, nursing a sore knee, Orr was back to lead the Bruins to another Cup win—this time over the New York Rangers in the finals.

⬤ **Ever heard of Chris Hayes?** His name is on the Stanley Cup. In 1972, when the Bruins won the Stanley Cup over the St. Louis Blues, Chris Hayes was called up for a game and earned a few seconds of precious ice time for the Bruins. That was it. He never played in a regular season game that season and never played again in the NHL after 1972. He is one of the most obscure forwards ever to have his name engraved on the Cup.

⬤ **Half a dozen years** after the NHL doubled in size in 1967, the Philadelphia Flyers became the first expansion team to win the Stanley Cup. They defeated Bobby Orr and the Boston Bruins in six games in 1974. The Flyers made it two Cups in a row the following season, defeating Buffalo in the finals. The parades that followed those two victories were the biggest in history.

⬤ **In one of those** playoff games between the Flyers and the Sabres, the fog was so thick in the Buffalo Memorial Auditorium the players could barely see the puck—or each other. I kept yelling at them, "I'm over here, guys!" Goaltender Bernie Parent was named playoff MVP in both 1974 and 1975.

● **Fred "The Fog" Shero** was the coach of the Philadelphia Flyers when they won the Stanley Cup in 1974 and 1975. Before leading his team to a clinching game 6 victory over the Boston Bruins in the 1974 Stanley Cup final, the team's first-ever Stanley Cup, Fred Shero wrote an oft-quoted motivational line on the team's blackboard: "Win together today, and we walk together forever." Another of his utterances drew some chuckles. From behind the Flyers' bench one night, in a game against the Islanders, he pointed at a player. "Who's number 18?" he asked. "That's Eddie Westfall," a player told him. "No, no," he said. "Number 18 on our team."

Shero was also the coach of the New York Rangers when they reached the Stanley Cup Finals in 1979.

Coach Shero died of cancer on November 24, 1990, at the age of 65. In a 1999 Philadelphia newspaper poll, Fred Shero was selected as the city's greatest professional coach/manager, beating out legends such as Connie Mack of baseball's Athletics, Dallas Green of baseball's Phillies, Dick Vermeil and Greasy Neale of the NFL's Philadelphia Eagles, and Billy Cunningham and Alex Hannum of the NBA's Philadelphia 76ers.

● **Has there ever been** a team with a winning tradition like the Montreal Canadiens from 1975 through 1979? Those Habs were almost invincible. Let's look at their regular season records:

Season	Wins	Losses	Ties
1975–76	58	11	11
1976–77	60	8	12
1977–78	59	10	11
1978–79	52	17	11

In the playoffs, they were near perfect, winning the Cup in 1976 with a 12–1 record. In 1977, they went 12–2; in 1978, it was 12–3; and in 1979, they were 12–4. Four Stanley Cups in four years with a playoff record of 48–10. And they might have won five straight Cups if goalie Ken Dryden hadn't retired and coach Scotty Bowman hadn't been lured away to Buffalo.

● **The New York Islanders** became the dominant NHL team in the early 1980s. Manager Bill Torrey's club won four consecutive Stanley Cups from 1980 to 1983. But they couldn't have done it without Mike Bossy's sniping. Islander fans shuddered to think that Bossy might easily have become a Hab, not an Isle. Montreal coach Scotty Bowman urged manager Sam Pollock to draft Bossy in 1977, but Pollock listened to his scouts, who thought Bossy was a soft player. He opted for Mark Napier instead. Bossy enjoyed a Hall of Fame career with the Islanders, scoring 573 career goals.

In 1981–82, Bossy was the fastest player to reach 300 goals in the number of games played, as well as the fastest player to reach 500 goals in the number of games played in 1985–86, only to have both goal marks surpassed and scored faster by Wayne Gretzky's 300 goals in 1983–84 and 500 in 1986–87. Bossy is the third-fastest player to reach the 500-goal mark in the number of games played (647), behind only Wayne Gretzky's 500 goals in 575 games and Mario Lemieux's 500 goals in 605 games.

During their glory years, the New York Islanders became the first American team to win four consecutive Stanley Cups and they put together a string of 19 consecutive play-off series victories—a pro sports record.

⬤ **How did this happen?** Hockey fans rubbed their eyes in disbelief when the lowly Los Angeles Kings, in 17th place, eliminated the powerful second-place Edmonton Oilers in the first round of the 1982 playoffs. The teams set a playoff record of 18 goals in the opener, which was won by the Kings 10–8.

Game three turned out to be one of the most incredible in NHL history and would be given its own moniker—the "Miracle on Manchester" (the Kings arena, the Forum, was on Manchester Boulevard). In that game, played on April 10, 1982, Wayne Gretzky dazzled early and paced the Oilers to a commanding 5–0 lead after two periods. Kings fans resigned themselves to a blowout loss. But the Kings stunned the crowd—and the Oilers—with an unbelievable comeback in the third period, tying the score on a goal by left winger Steve Bozek at 19:55 of the third period and sending the game into overtime. At 2:35 in the overtime period, Kings left winger Daryl Evans fired a slapshot off a faceoff in the right circle and beat Oilers goalie Grant Fuhr to give the Kings an incredible come-from-behind overtime victory, 6–5. People still talk about that barnburner.

Not only did the Kings mesmerize the vaunted Oilers, but they also went on to topple them from the playoffs when the Kings captured the series three games to two. In regular season play, the Kings had won only 24 games to the Oilers' 48. Oilers fans were livid, and sports columnist Terry Jones roasted the team in the *Edmonton Journal*: "From today until they've won a playoff series again, they are weak-kneed wimps who thought they were God's gift to the NHL but found out they were nothing but adolescent, front-running, good-time Charlies who couldn't handle any adversity."

Somehow I doubt that Jones was invited to the Oilers' season-ending party. But then, neither was I.

⬤ **When the Montreal Canadiens** beat the Calgary Flames to win the Stanley Cup in 1986, rookie goalie Patrick Roy was the hero and the Conn Smythe Trophy winner. Roy became the first rookie in 31 years to chalk up a shutout in the final series. But while the Habs were celebrating their Cup win in Calgary, things turned ugly back in Montreal. A celebration turned into a riot. Fans broke windows, over-turned cars, and looted stores in the downtown area. They lit a huge bonfire, and when a fire truck arrived, they attacked it. A riot squad eventually restored order.

⬤ **In a 1987** playoff series at Montreal between the Habs and the Flyers, game six is remembered for an astonishing pregame brawl. The Habs had a ritual of shooting the puck into their opponent's empty net after the teams finished their warmup before the game. On this night, Flyer tough guy Ed Hospodar and backup goalie Chico Resch were determined to stop them. When the Habs' Shane Corson and Claude Lemieux moved in to take the empty net shot, Hospodar rushed across the ice and hooked Corson while Resch threw his goal stick to block the shot. That did it! Within seconds, players from both clubs were involved in a battle that lasted 10 minutes. Following the game, NHL executive vice-president Brian O'Neill assessed fines total-ling $24,000 to the players involved in the fight and Hospodar was suspended for the balance of the playoffs.

⬤ **Have you ever seen** a person run out on the ice in the middle of a Stanley Cup playoff game? I have. It happened in Calgary in 1989 in game two of a playoff series between the Flames and the Kings. When Flames goaltender Mike Vernon was knocked flat by the Kings' Bernie Nicholls, the referee signalled a delayed penalty. Calgary's colourful trainer, Bearcat Murray, didn't hesitate. He jumped the boards and raced to Vernon's side. Meanwhile, play carried into the Kings' zone and Calgary scored. The referee signalled a goal. Wayne Gretzky, captain of the Kings, was furious. "You can't allow a goal when their trainer was on the ice," he protested. But the goal stood, and Calgary went on to win the Stanley Cup that spring. Murray likes to say, "I was plus one in the playoffs that year."

● **In 1997,** the Detroit Red Wings, after defeating the St. Louis Blues, the Mighty Ducks of Anaheim, and the Colorado Avalanche in the first three rounds, went on to wallop the Philadelphia Flyers in four straight games in the Stanley Cup finals. It was Detroit's first Stanley Cup since 1955, breaking the longest drought—42 years long—in the league at that time. Goalie Mike Vernon was named the Conn Smythe Trophy winner as the most valuable player.

In the following week, defenceman Vladimir Konstantinov suffered a brain injury in a limo accident and his career came to an abrupt end. The Red Wings dedicated the 1997–98 season, which also ended in a Stanley Cup, to Konstantinov, who came out onto the ice in his wheelchair. The Wings won in another sweep, this time over the Washington Capitals. It was Chris Osgood in goal for all four games in the 1998 finals, while Steve Yzerman won the Conn Smythe.

The Wings also posted the league's best record in the 2001–02 regular season and defeated Colorado in seven games in the Western Conference finals after beating the Vancouver Canucks and St. Louis Blues in rounds one and two. The Red Wings went on to capture another Stanley Cup in five games over the Carolina Hurricanes, with Nicklas Lidstrom winning the Conn Smythe Trophy.

Coach Scotty Bowman and goalie Dominik Hasek both retired after the season.

● **How about** Dave Andreychuk's long wait? In 2003–04, playing for Tampa Bay, Andreychuk was about to end 22 seasons of play in the NHL—with no Stanley Cup win in sight. No player in history had played more games without gripping the old mug.

Then Brad Richards put together one of the all-time clutch performances in playoff history, potting seven game-winning goals, while goalie Nikolai Khabibulin posted a 16–7 record with five shutouts and a sparkling 1.71 goals-against average. Tampa Bay made it to the finals against the Calgary Flames. The series went to a seventh game played in Tampa Bay. The Flames scored one goal on Khabibulin, but that was all. The Lightning scored twice and won 2–1. Andreychuk was finally able to kiss the Cup. He retired midway through his 23rd season. I say any player who scores 640 career goals in the NHL deserves to sip from the Cup at least once.

● **On June 4, 2008,** the Red Wings, now coached by Mike Babcock, won their 11th Stanley Cup—which was also their fourth in 11 years. It was also the first time a team captained by a non-North-American player—Nicklas Lidstrom—won the Stanley Cup. The final victory came against the Pittsburgh Penguins, by a score of 3–2. Henrik Zetterberg scored the winning goal in the decisive game 6 and was named the winner of the Conn Smythe Trophy.

● **Mario Lemieux,** as the principal owner of the 2009 Stanley Cup champion Pittsburgh Penguins, is the only person to win the Cup as a player and an owner. Lemieux saved the Penguins from bankruptcy in 1999 following a brilliant career that current Penguin superstar Sidney Crosby will be hard pressed to match. Lemieux won two Stanley Cups, an Olympic gold medal, a Canada Cup, and a World Cup. He won three Hart Trophies as the NHL's MVP, six Art Ross Trophies as leading scorer, and two Conn Smythe Trophies as playoff MVP. Whenever Mario cradled me on his stick, I knew where I'd wind up—in the other team's net!

● **Former coach** Scotty Bowman has lots of Stanley Cup memories. He should have. He's won the old mug more times than any other coach. Here are a few of his stories:

> The first Cup we won in Montreal was in 1973. We won the Cup in May, and our baby was due around that time. When we had a boy, born in June, we decided to name him Stanley. We named him Stanley Glenn—Glenn after Glenn Hall, our goalie in St. Louis. So our newborn son got a real hockey name. When he was young, we always called him Stanley Cup. Now a few years go by and one day I was in some office filling in some forms. Stanley was with me, waiting while I filled in all the family names. When we left, I noticed that Stanley was really glum. I said, "What's wrong, son?" and he said, "Dad, is my name not Stanley Cup anymore?"
>
> I reassured him as best I could. I said, "Son, your name will always be Stanley Cup to us."

> Remember, the owners and managers want to see their names on the Cup, too.
>
> When we won in Pittsburgh in '91, some of our

scouts were disappointed. There was no room for them. And yet—get this—our strength conditioning coach, who nobody really knows, got his name on the Cup, with 'strength conditioning coach' engraved after it. His title took up a whole line.

A unique thing happened to Stanley that year. He was at college at Notre Dame and he took a couple of days off to come to Chicago to see Pittsburgh play the Blackhawks. When we swept the series, after game four, he slipped out on the ice and was part of the victory celebration. That's something he'll never forget.

And in 2010, as general manager of the Chicago Blackhawks, he helped with the trophy he's named after.

● **Check it out, fans.** A few Stanley Cup playoff records you'll find intriguing:

- Most Stanley Cups as a player: Henri Richard, Montreal Canadiens, 11 (1956 to 1960, 1965, 1966, 1968, 1969, 1971, 1973)
- Most Stanley Cups as a non-player: Sam Pollock, Montreal Canadiens, 12 (1959, 1960, 1965–1966, 1968, 1969, 1971, 1973, 1976–1979)
- Most Stanley Cups as either a player or non-player: Jean Béliveau, Montreal Canadiens, 17. Béliveau's name appears on the Stanley Cup the most (as player: 1956–60, 1965, 1966, 1968, 1969, 1971; as executive: 1973, 1976–79, 1986, 1993)

● **Some players** will do anything to win the Cup. In 1983, when the Edmonton Oilers faced off against the New York

Islanders in the finals, goalie Billy Smith of the Isles was the man in the spotlight. In game one, Smith slashed Oiler Glenn Anderson across the knee. In game two, he chopped down Wayne Gretzky when the league's top scorer tried to bring the puck out from behind the net. In game three, he didn't slash anybody, but in game four, he collided with Anderson in the goal crease, and when Anderson's stick grazed Smith's helmet, he tumbled to the ice, writhing in pain. The referee gave Anderson a five-minute penalty. Smith promptly jumped to his feet. The Isles won the series in four games and Smith admitted on *Hockey Night in Canada* he'd taken a dive. In front of NHL president John Ziegler, who'd just handed him the Conn Smythe Trophy, Smith said, "Sure I planned the dive. I rolled around on the ice like Gretzky did when I hit him. He laid down and cried. So I took a chapter out of his book. Two can play at that game." Smith's bitter words and public admission of his deceit infuriated many TV viewers. But they had to admit his goaltending in the series had been remarkable.

⬤ **In the spring** of 1988, the Detroit Red Wings met the Edmonton Oilers in the Campbell Conference finals. The winning team would go on to play in the Stanley Cup finals.

The Oilers required only five games to put the Red Wings away. But several of the Wings lost more than a season-ending series. Detroit owner Mike Ilitch had promised each of his players a significant bonus—$16,000 (matching the playoff bonus money they had already earned) if they performed well against the Oilers.

But when he discovered that, the night before the final game in the series, six of his Red Wings had broken a strict curfew established by coach Jacques Demers, he was furious. All six night owls—Bob Probert, Darren Veitch, John

Chabot, Joey Kocur, Darren Elliot, and Petr Klima—had been seen imbibing at a nightclub long after they should have been back in their hotel rooms.

Breaking club rules proved to be very costly to the guilty Wings. Ilitch said, "Sorry, boys. You just lost your bonus money of $16,000. I hope the fun you had was worth it. What's more, some of you won't be around when another season gets under way." The rest of the Red Wings received the additional cash from the generous owner.

In the finals, Edmonton defeated Boston in four straight games to win their fourth Stanley Cup in five seasons.

● **On June 12, 2009,** Sidney Crosby of the Pittsburgh Penguins became the youngest captain in NHL history to win the Stanley Cup and on the same day his teammate, Evgeni Malkin became the first Russian player in NHL history to win the Conn Smythe Trophy as the MVP of the 2009 playoffs.

● **The 2010 playoffs** saw a huge early upset. Montreal goalie Jaraslav Halak made 41 saves in a spectacular game seven performance, and his teammates combined to block a whopping 41 shots when eighth-seeded Montreal held on to beat Washington 2–1, stunning the Presidents' Trophy winners by reeling off three consecutive victories to take the first-round series four games to three. The Canadiens became the ninth number eight team to knock off a number one in 32 matchups since the NHL went to its current playoff format in 1994—and the first to come back from a 3–1 series deficit.

● **Halak, the 25-year-old** Slovakian goalie, was equally spectacular in the second round, leading Montreal to a four games to one ouster of the Pittsburgh Penguins, defending Stanley Cup champions. But the Philadelphia Flyers dashed the Habs' hopes with a 4–1 series victory in round three of the playoffs. As for Halak, he was traded to St. Louis after the season.

Some Fabulous Hockey Records . . . and a Few Less Memorable Ones

● **Players and teams** have set some amazing records in hockey. They've also established some that are downright embarrassing. Like the Chicago Black Hawks, for example, who set records for futility in 1928–29 that have lasted for more than 80 years. In their third NHL season, the Black Hawks won a mere seven games in a 44-game schedule. During one eight-game stretch, they were shut out eight straight times. They couldn't get me over the other team's goal line—not even once. Over the course of the season, the Hawks were blanked 21 times, or almost 50 per cent of the time. And their so-called scorers were pitiful, managing only 33 goals all season, less than one per game. Forward Vic Ripley led the Hawk scorers with 11 goals and 2 assists for 13 points, a woeful total for a club's leading scorer. The Hawks' second-leading scorer was Johnny Gottselig, who tallied five goals and three assists for eight points. I remember when Wayne Gretzky and Mario Lemieux would score that many points in a weekend. That season, the Hawks had Charlie Gardiner in goal or they might not have won a single game. Gardiner happened to be among the league's best netminders, posting five shutouts and a 1.93 goals-against average in 44 games.

● **Years later,** a Chicago player set a brilliant record in the final game of the 1951–52 season. It's a mark that still

stands. Forward Bill Mosienko scored three goals in 21 seconds against rookie Rangers netminder Lorne Anderson.
Gus Bodnar assisted on all three of Mosienko's goals to
establish a record for the three fastest assists. And Anderson
never played another NHL game.

● **Despite the fact** he was blind in one eye, One-Eyed
Frank McGee averaged nearly three goals per game during
his career with Ottawa. In a Stanley Cup match in 1905
against Dawson City, McGee scored a record 14 goals
against 17-year-old netminder Albert Forrest. McGee was
killed in action in France during World War I.

● **On March 5, 1912,** Frank Patrick set a record in hockey
that may last forever. While playing for Vancouver against
New Westminster in the Pacific Coast Hockey League, he
scored six goals in one night, playing on defence. He
achieved this remarkable total through some quite amazing rink-length dashes and despite the fact he was playing
with an injured eye. The opposing goaltender was the renowned Hughie Lehman, possessor of the best goals-against
average in the league.

● **Toronto's Babe Dye** won the 1920–21 NHL goal-
scoring title with 35 goals in 24 games. However, he collected
a mere five assists, the lowest ever for a 30-goal scorer.

● **On January 31, 1920**, Joe Malone of the Quebec
Bulldogs set the all-time NHL record for goals in a game with
seven. Quebec walloped Toronto 19–6. In his career, Malone
pumped in 143 goals in 126 games, a pace that many modern-
day scoring wizards have not been able to match. Earlier that
season, Malone scored six goals in a game. Five other players

have scored six goals in a game, including brothers Corb and Cy Denneny, Syd Howe, Darryl Sittler, and Red Berenson.

● **During the 1921–22** season, Ottawa's Punch Broadbent potted goals in 16 consecutive games, establishing a record that has never been broken. The previous record holder was Joe Malone with 35 goals in 14 straight games in 1917–18.

● **On February 28, 1929,** the Chicago Black Hawks were shut out for the eighth straight time when they settled for a 0–0 tie with the visiting New York Americans (New York Rangers). Gosh, fellows, couldn't anybody put the biscuit in the basket?

● **On February 14, 1931,** the official scorer at Maple Leaf Gardens awarded three assists on a goal by Charlie Conacher. It was another NHL first. Assisting on Charlie's goal were King Clancy, Joe Primeau, and Busher Jackson. The Leafs tied Detroit 1–1. Not to be outdone, on January 10, 1935, the official scorer in New York awarded four assists on a goal by the Leafs' Joe Primeau in a game against the Rangers (Americans) that ended in a 5–5 tie.

● **On January 16, 1934,** tiny Ken Doraty of the Leafs scored the only overtime hat trick in NHL history when Toronto defeated the Senators 7–4 at Ottawa. At that time, overtime meant a full 10 minutes, not sudden death.

● **On March 4, 1941,** the Boston Bruins set a record with 83 shots in a game against Chicago netminder Sam LoPresti. Despite the barrage, LoPresti allowed only three goals in a 3–2 loss.

● **In 1942–43,** rookie Gus Bodnar of the Toronto Maple Leafs scored 22 goals and won the Calder Trophy as the NHL's top freshman. But his first goal was memorable. He scored just 15 seconds from the opening faceoff in his first game against the New York Rangers. Only Dave Christian of the 1980 Winnipeg Jets scored a faster goal on his first shift in his first game. He zapped me into the net in seven seconds.

● **New York Rangers** fans become enraged when their team goes into a lengthy slump. You can imagine how they reacted during World War II. During the 1942–43 season, the Rangers went 19 games without a win. The following year, they started with a 15-game winless streak and finished 6–39–5, allowing more than six goals per game.

● **The most lopsided game** in U.S. college history took place in 1944. Dartmouth College walloped Middlebury College 30–0, with Dick Rondeau scoring 12 goals and adding 11 assists for 23 points. After Rondeau's outburst, they should have called it Middle Buried College.

● **Maurice "Rocket" Richard** was the fiery captain of the Montreal Canadiens when they captured a record five consecutive Stanley Cups from 1956 to 1960. He was the first NHL player to score 50 goals in 50 games and the first to score 500 career goals. Idolized by millions, he set the scoring standards that inspired other Habs: Jean Béliveau, Bernie Geoffrion, Steve Shutt, and Guy Lafleur. It's only fitting that in 1998, the NHL named the Maurice Richard Trophy in his honour, to be awarded each season to the league's top goal scorer.

● **Folks, when I made** my TV debut in the seventies, Boston's Bobby Orr was the most electrifying player in hockey. Before Orr came along, hockey people thought it was impossible for a defenceman to win the individual scoring title in the NHL. In 1969–70, Bobby amazed everyone by finishing on top of the scoring race with 120 points, 21 more than teammate Phil Esposito. No defenceman had ever come close to winning a scoring title. It was unthinkable. Bobby finished on top again five years later, this time with 135 points. What many fans forget is that he played for most of his career on aching knees—knees that had required numerous operations.

● **On March 29, 1970,** Chicago's rookie goalie, Tony Esposito, recorded his 15th shutout of the season—a modern-day record.

● **On December 21, 1975,** the Buffalo Sabres set the NHL record for most points by one team in a game when they pummelled Washington 14–2. The Sabres were credited with 26 assists for a point total of 40.

● **On February 2, 1977,** Toronto's Ian Turnbull set a record for defencemen when he scored five goals in a game in a 9–1 rout of Detroit. Turnbull took five shots on goal and scored on all of them.

● **In 1977–78,** the Boston Bruins set a record for the most 20-goal scorers on one team—11. Rookie Bob Miller made the mark possible when he scored his 20th on the next-to-last night of the year.

⬤ **In all of major pro sports,** the longest undefeated streak belongs to the 1979–80 Philadelphia Flyers. It was a streak that began in October and lasted through December. After losing the second game of the season to Atlanta, the Flyers topped Toronto 4–3, and that was the beginning of a remarkable romp around the NHL. When the streak reached 28 games, the Flyers tied the NHL record, held by the Montreal Canadiens. Two nights later, they set a new mark of 29 with a win over Boston. In December, they snapped the pro sports record of 33 games established by basketball's Los Angeles Lakers. The end came for the Flyers in game 36 when they were walloped 7–1 by Minnesota. Three decades later, the Flyers' record of 25 wins and 10 ties still stands.

● **On March 11, 1979,** at the Philadelphia Spectrum, Randy Holt of the Los Angeles Kings racked up nine penalties totalling 67 minutes—an NHL record. He collected one minor, three majors, two 10-minute misconducts, and three game misconducts—all in the first period. Frank Bathe, the Flyer who scrapped with Holt several times in the opening frame, finished the game with 55 penalty minutes, the second-highest single game total ever.

You know what I always say. You can't hurt the opposing team if you're sitting in the penalty box.

● **What a race it was** between Ray Bourque and Paul Coffey for the title of highest-scoring defenceman in history! Bourque ended his career with 410 goals and 1,579 points. Coffey was a close second with 396 goals and 1,531 points. I wonder how long it will be before another high-scoring defenceman will match those numbers.

● **During the 1983–84** season, the Edmonton Oilers scored a record 446 goals. During a stretch of five seasons in that era, they were the only team to score over 400 goals each year. In 1983–84, the Oilers boasted a record three 50-plus-goal scorers: Wayne Gretzky (87), Glenn Anderson (54), and Jari Kurri (52). Two seasons later, they tied the record with Kurri (68), Anderson (54), and Gretzky (52).

● **On December 31, 1988,** Mario Lemieux of the Penguins scored five goals—one on the power play, one shorthanded, one at even strength, one on a penalty shot, and one into an empty net. When he couldn't think of another way to score, he settled for three assists in an 8–6 victory over the New Jersey Devils. And I say it may be a hundred years before that happens again.

● **Doug Jarvis,** who played with Montreal, Washington, and Hartford, holds the NHL record for most consecutive games played. From October 8, 1975, through October 10, 1987, Jarvis played in 964 games. If hockey had a report card for attendance, I'd give Jarvis an A+.

● **Garry Unger,** who played with Toronto, Detroit, St. Louis, Atlanta, and Edmonton and scored over 400 career goals, holds the second-longest consecutive game streak with 914. But the record Garry set that impresses *me* came after his NHL career, when he played a couple of seasons in England. In 1985–86, in 35 games with the Dundee Rockets, he tallied 86 goals and 48 assists for 134 points. The following year, in 30 games with the Peterborough Pirates, he scored 95 goals and 143 assists for 238 points. And get this, kids: Unger might have spent his entire career with the Detroit Red Wings, but coach Ned Harkness didn't like his shoulder-length hair, so he traded him to the Blues. In St. Louis, Unger was an All-Star choice for seven straight years.

● **When Wayne Gretzky** retired, he held a total of 61 NHL records. He is the only NHL player to collect over 200 points in a season—and he did it four times. His highest point total came in 1985–86, when he amassed 215. Mario Lemieux almost reached 200 points in 1988–89 but fell one point short and finished with 199.

● **On March 23, 1994,** Gretzky of the Kings scored career goal 802 to pass Gordie Howe and establish a new NHL record for most career goals. The Great One finished his career with a record 894 goals, 93 more than Howe.

● **During his career,** Gretzky had 50 three-or-more-goal games. In 20 seasons, he amassed 37 three-goal games, nine four-goal games, and four five-goal games. Mario Lemieux had 40 three-or-more-goal games, while Mike Bossy had 39.

● **Gretzky also holds** the record for the longest consecutive point-scoring streak in the NHL. In a 51 game streak during the 1983–84 season, Gretzky scored 61 goals and added 92 assists for 153 points.

● **Dave Andreychuk,** who played for 23 seasons and with six different teams, holds the record for most power play goals in a career—274.

● **The NHL record** for the fastest goal from the start of a game is five seconds. Three players share the mark: Doug Smail (Winnipeg Jets, 1981), Bryan Trottier (New York Islanders, 1984), and Alexander Mogilny (Buffalo Sabres, 1991).

● **On December 19, 1987,** the Bruins' Ken Linesman and the Blues' Doug Gilmour scored goals just two seconds apart to set an NHL record for the fastest two goals in a game. Gilmour's goal came off a centre ice faceoff and was scored into an empty net.

● **In 1988–89,** Mario Lemieux scored or assisted on 199 of Pittsburgh's 347 goals. That's 57.2 of them—an all-time high.

● **In 1990,** the closest vote in history for the Hart Trophy saw Edmonton's Mark Messier nose out Boston's Ray

Bourque by two votes, 227 to 225. Incredibly, Wayne Gretzky, who had captured nine of the past 10 Harts, received a single vote. Gretzky took home the Art Ross Trophy as scoring champ.

● **During their initial** NHL season, 1974–75, the Washington Capitals shattered a modern-day record for futility with a record of eight wins, 67 losses, and five ties. In one 11-game stretch, they were shut out five times. They established a record for consecutive losses with 17 and another mark for losses on the road with 37. The team went through three coaches: Jim Anderson (54 games), Red Sullivan (19 games), and Milt Schmidt (seven games). In 1992–93, the Ottawa Senators lost one more road game than the Caps to establish a new mark of 40. And the San Jose Sharks during the same season established a new record for losses with 71.

● **It's unusual for** an NHL player to take more than 400 shots on goal during a season. Only four players have done it: Paul Kariya, Alex Ovechkin, Bobby Hull, and Phil Esposito. Esposito did it twice and is the only player to take more than 500 shots. In 1970–71, Espo fired a record 550 shots on goal.

● **Dave "Tiger" Williams** ended his 14-season career in the NHL as the game's most penalized player. Williams served 3,966 minutes of penalty time. Runner-up Dale Hunter, who played 19 seasons, finished with 3,565 penalty minutes. What naughty boys they were!

● **During a game** against Hartford in 1991, Boston's Chris Nilan spent more time in the penalty box than he did on the ice. He served six minors, two majors, one 10-minute misconduct, and one game misconduct for a record total of 10 penalties in a single game.

● **In 1976,** Leaf captain Darryl Sittler scored six goals and collected four assists for a record 10-point night in a game against the Boston Bruins and rookie goalie Dave Reece. Sittler's 10-point output has never been matched. As for Reece, it was his final game in the NHL.

● **Here's a record** every hockey player would like to own: most Stanley Cup wins. It belongs to Henri Richard of the Montreal Canadiens. He retired with 11 Stanley Cup championships. Some players have retired after 20 seasons without a single one. And get this. Richard was a leap year baby, so he had more Cup rings than he had birthdays. He celebrated only nine birthdays during his amateur and pro career.

● **Here's an easy question:** Can you name hockey's oldest and most successful team? Of course you can. It's the Montreal Canadiens, who celebrated their 100th birthday in 2009. In 1993, the Montreal Canadiens captured their 24th Stanley Cup, defeating the Los Angeles Kings in a five-game series. During the '93 playoffs, the Canadiens won a record 10 straight games in overtime. Montreal goalie Patrick Roy, who posted a 16–4 record, was awarded the Conn Smythe Trophy as playoff MVP.

● **The 1992–93** season ended with the greatest number of 50-goal, 60-goal, and 100-point scorers in NHL history. Fourteen players reached the 50-goal plateau, four more than the previous mark of 10 set in 1981–82; five players scored at least 60 goals, two more than the old standard of three established in 1988–89; and 21 players reached the 100 point-mark, topping the previous mark of 16 set in 1984–85.

● **Mike Bossy** joined the Islanders in 1977–78 and scored 50 goals in his rookie season—the first rookie to accomplish this feat. And it was no fluke. For nine straight seasons, he scored 50 or more goals and five times he topped 60. One year, he scored 50 goals in 50 games. Sadly, in his 10th season, back problems slowed him down and he was forced to retire. You were one of the greatest, Mike. And with three Lady Byngs in your trophy case, one of the most gentlemanly players in the game.

● **Wayne Gretzky** won the Hart Trophy a record nine times during his career, eight consecutively. He has been named MVP more times than any other player in the history of the other three North American major professional leagues (Major League Baseball, the National Basketball Association, and the National Football League).

● **Rookie players** in the NHL are often nervous and apprehensive. And who can blame them? But many rise to the occasion and have outstanding rookie seasons. Take a look at the following records and see if you don't agree.

- Most goals by a rookie, one season: Teemu Selanne (1992–93), 76.
- Most goals by a player in his first NHL season, one game: Howie Meeker (January 8, 1947) and Don Murdoch (October 12, 1976), both with 5.
- Most goals by a player in his first NHL game: Alex Smart (January 14, 1943), Réal Cloutier (October 10, 1979), and Fabian Brunnström (October 16, 2008), all with 3.
- Most assists by a rookie, one season: Peter Stastny (1980–81) and Joe Juneau (1992–93), both with 70. (Wayne Gretzky had 86 assists in 1979–80 but was not considered a rookie because of his single season in the WHA when he was 17.)
- Most assists by a player in his first NHL season, one game: Wayne Gretzky (February 15, 1980), 7.
- Most assists by a player in his first NHL game: Dutch Reibel (October 8, 1953) and Roland Eriksson (October 6, 1977), both with 4.
- Most points by a rookie, one season: Teemu Selanne (1992–93), 132. (Wayne Gretzky had 137 points in

1979–80 but was not considered a rookie because of his season in the WHA.)

- Most points by a player in his first NHL season, one game: Peter and Anton Stastny (February 22, 1981), 8 each.
- Most points by a player in his first NHL game: Al Hill (February 14, 1977), 5.
- Most goals by a rookie defenceman, one season: Brian Leetch (1988–89), 23.
- Most assists by a rookie defenceman, one season: Larry Murphy (1980–81), 60.
- Most points by a rookie defenceman, one season: Larry Murphy (1980–81), 76.
- Longest goal-scoring streak to start a career (pre-modern): Joe Malone (1917–1918), 14 games.
- Longest goal-scoring streak to start a career (modern): Evgeni Malkin (2006–07), 6 games.
- Longest point streak by a rookie, one season: Paul Stastny (February 3, 2007, to March 17, 2007), 20 games.

On March 12, 2009, New York Ranger goalie Henrik Lundqvist became the first goaltender in NHL history to win 30 games in each of his first four seasons. Three weeks later, Curtis Joseph, goaltender with the Toronto Maple Leafs, lost his 352nd game, tying him with Gump Worsley for most losses by a goaltender.

When Coaches Lose Their Cool

● **One of hockey'**s most colourful coaches was Don "Grapes" Cherry, now a TV star on *Hockey Night in Canada*. When Cherry coached in Colorado, he blew up one night and grabbed one of his defencemen by the throat. "I gave him a little shake," Grapes told me, "because he wouldn't do what I asked him to."

● **When Cherry's Rockies** played in Boston one night, during a time-out he agreed to sign several autographs for fans who approached the Colorado bench. I'd never seen that happen before.

● **Cherry often talks** about his minor league American Hockey League coach in Springfield, Eddie Shore. Among his observations:

- Springfield players were instructed by Shore never to tip a cab driver more than 15 cents. As a result, cabbies tried to avoid picking up hockey players.
- At contract time, Shore would grant a player bonus money for scoring 30 goals. But when the player reached 29 goals, he was likely to find himself riding the bench for the rest of the season.

- If one of his goalies flopped to the ice too often in work-outs, Shore would get a rope and tie him to the crossbar.
- Shore needed goaltending help one season and traded for a player named Smith. When Smith arrived, Shore asked, "Where are your goal pads?" Smith answered, "Mr. Shore, I'm not a goalie, I'm a left winger."
- One player traded to Springfield arrived in time to see the team working out in a hotel lobby. They were prac-tising dance routines.
- Springfield's "Black Aces" were players who were in Shore's doghouse. They practised but seldom played. They were required to paint the arena seats, sell pro-grams at games, make popcorn, and blow up balloons for special events.

● **Can you imagine** a coach in the NHL engaging in fisticuffs with a referee? Such a battle broke out on the night of March 14, 1933, at the Boston Garden during the overtime of a game between the Bruins and the Black Hawks. The incident occurred shortly after Boston went ahead 3–2 after three minutes of overtime, which in those days was not sudden death but required a full 10 minutes of extra play. When Boston forward Marty Barry scored, Chicago manager/coach Tommy Gorman was furious. He was certain that the puck had not crossed the goal line. When referee Bill Stewart skated near the Chicago bench, Gorman grabbed him by the jersey and began throwing punches at the startled official. The crowd roared when Stewart, a much smaller man, began punching right back.

Finally, Stewart broke free of Gorman's flailing fists and ordered the manager to the dressing room. When Gorman refused to budge, several husky policemen moved in and dragged him down the corridor. One by one, the

Chicago players left the ice and followed Gorman to the dressing room. Some of them began to argue with the police and were threatened with a night in jail if they didn't behave.

Referee Stewart skated to centre ice and pulled out his watch. He'd give the Hawks exactly 60 seconds to get a line-up back on the ice. When his ultimatum was ignored, he forfeited the match to the Bruins. It was the first time in NHL history that a coach and referee exchanged punches and the first time a team left the ice with the outcome still in doubt. Referee Stewart said the penalty for such a breach of the rules meant forfeiting two points and a $1,000 fine.

● **By the end** of the 1948–49 NHL season, Toronto coach Clarence "Hap" Day had an enviable coaching record in hockey—in fact, a record-breaking one. In nine seasons behind the Leaf bench, he had captured five Stanley Cups.

In 1941–42, his Leafs made history by losing the first three games of the final series to Detroit, then stormed back to take four in a row to capture the Cup.

In 1944–45 Day used only "eleven good men and true" to end the Montreal Canadiens' reign.

Then came his grand slam feat with victories in '47, '48 and '49.

If the Leafs had won again in 1950, Day might have been the first coach to lead his team to five consecutive Cup triumphs, because Toronto won again in 1951 on Bill Barilko's memorable overtime goal. But Day's Leafs finished third in the standings in 1949–50, behind second-place Montreal and first-place Detroit. The Wings' big line of Lindsay, Abel, and Howe finished one-two-three in the scoring race, with Lindsay taking the Art Ross Trophy. The Leafs trounced Detroit 5–0 in the opening game of the semifinals, a game in which Howe suffered a devastating injury. When Ted Kennedy slipped away from a Howe check, the big right winger slammed head first into the boards and suffered a concussion, a broken nose, a scratched eyeball, and a broken cheekbone. Despite the loss of Howe, the Wings fought back and eliminated Toronto in seven games. They went on to edge the Rangers in the finals.

By then, Hap Day had had enough of the pressures of coaching. He quit as the Leaf mentor in 1950 but stayed with the team for another seven years as an assistant manager and manager. But he wasn't happy in the role. His self-esteem suffered working for Conn Smythe, who made most of the major decisions. Day was never comfortable playing a subservient position, so he resigned for good in 1957.

Day was one of the toughest coaches ever to handle the Leafs. His training camps were described as prison camps. Pity the poor Leaf who made mistakes in practice. Day would jump all over him. He believed in defensive hockey, and opponents complained that his Leafs were nothing more than clutch and grab artists.

● **When Roger Neilson** coached a junior hockey team in Peterborough, and pulled his goalie for an extra attacker in the dying seconds of a game, he instructed him to leave his goal stick on the ice in front of the net. If the opposing team took a long shot at the empty net, Neilson hoped that the goal stick would stop the puck. The league quickly brought in a new rule to block such a move.

● **One night,** when he was coaching the Peterborough juniors, before a playoff game against London, Neilson anticipated needing a few delays during the game, some "breathers" to give his top players a moment's rest. So he secretly handed some of the Peterborough junior B players, who were seated in the stands, some eggs to throw on the ice at the appropriate time. Whenever Neilson tugged on his ear, three or four eggs were to be tossed on the ice, the referee would blow his whistle, and there'd be a nice long delay while the gooey mess was cleaned up. But Neilson forgot one important factor. He neglected to let the junior B coach in on his strategy. When the B coach arrived at the game midway through the contest and caught his players throwing eggs over the boards, he was outraged.

He was so angry he rounded them up and turfed them out. "Go home! Learn to behave yourselves," he thundered.

Soon there was a time when Neilson's top players needed another few minutes to catch their breath. He tugged on his ear. No eggs flew overhead. So he tugged again, harder. Still no eggs. The coach looked over his shoulder to discover a row of empty seats. His egg throwers had disappeared.

Undaunted, Neilson came up with a better system for the next game. This time, he handed the team trainer the eggs and ordered him to hide behind the boards at rinkside. When Neilson tugged on his ear, the trainer was to lob an egg or two onto the ice. But when the referee made a call that went against the Petes, the trainer let emotion get the better of him. He stood up and fired a couple of eggs right at the ref. He was caught red-handed and thrown out of the rink for his rash behaviour. Again, Neilson was left with no eggs and no one to throw them.

● **In junior hockey,** Neilson even employed his dog, Jacques, as an assistant coach. When a player started a rush from behind the net, Jacques would rush over and head him off, forcing him to turn back. "That's what I want you forwards to do," Neilson would say.

● **When he coached** the Buffalo Sabres, Roger Neilson once threw sticks and a water bottle on the ice to show his disdain for the officiating. Mike Milbury did the same thing when he coached a minor league club. His wife told him, "I thought you were going to throw some of your third-rate players over the boards as well." Another time, Milbury left the bench to run up to the organ loft to admonish the organist for playing a number Milbury thought was disrespectful to one of his players.

● **Tom Webster,** coach of the L. A. Kings, hurled a hockey stick, javelin style, at a referee during an NHL game, hitting the official on the foot.

● **Billy Reay,** when he coached Buffalo in the AHL, once got into a fistfight with the team's announcer.

● **Murph Chamberlain,** another Buffalo coach, once threw a bucket of pucks on the ice while a game was in progress.

● **Jacques Demers** and Mike Keenan are two NHL coaches who were caught tossing pennies on the ice to create a time-out during games.

● **Mike Keenan,** when he coached St. Louis in 1995, refused to dress his team in new alternate jerseys because they looked so horrible.

● **Toe Blake** of the Montreal Canadiens once stormed across the ice and punched a referee. He was fined $2,000. You ask me, Blake should have been suspended as well.

● **Emile Francis** of the Rangers once scooted around the rink to tell a goal judge off. Fans intervened, Francis found himself in the middle of a battle, and his players had to climb over the high glass, leap into the throng, and rescue him.

● **Coach Ernie McLean** guided the New Westminster Bruins to the Memorial Cup in 1977. And he did it by bending the rules. Playing against a superior team, the Portland Winterhawks, McLean reached into the Portland bench when the referee wasn't looking, grabbed a water bottle, and hurled it at the ref. Spotting the Portland logo on the bottle, the ref assumed a Portland player or coach had thrown the bottle and handed out a penalty to Portland. McLean's team scored on the power play, won the game, and went on to win the series. In a follow-up series, New Westminster won the Memorial Cup.

I look at it this way. Coaches will do anything to win. But when they cheat or break the rules, it sets a bad example to players.

● **In 1982–83,** rookie coach Orval Tessier guided the Chicago Black Hawks to a first-place finish in the Norris Division. It was a stunning improvement. Tessier, at season's end, would be named coach of the year. But his career took a sudden nosedive in the playoffs. The Edmonton Oilers bounced Chicago from the Stanley Cup chase in four straight games. Livid with rage, Tessier told the media, "My players need 18 heart transplants." Those ill-chosen words would cost Tessier all the respect he'd earned with the media. Reporters began calling him Mount Orval, Lava Lips, and the Glowering Inferno. The Hawks plunged from 104 points to 68 points in a season and a half. Mount Orval was fired and never got a second chance to coach in the NHL.

● **During the 1988** Stanley Cup playoffs, in the first intermission of a game between the St. Louis Blues and the Chicago Blackhawks, Chicago coach Bob Murdoch called for a strategy meeting with his assistant coaches. They gathered in a small room next to the team dressing room. Murdoch, the last man in, slammed the door hard behind him. When the meeting broke up, none of the coaches could get the door open again. Nor could it be opened from the outside. An arena worker saved the day. Riding up on a forklift truck, he crashed his machine into the door and sent panels flying. The three coaches stumbled over the broken pieces, dusted themselves off, and returned sheepishly to their duties behind the Blackhawk bench.

● **In 1989–90,** players with the junior Tri-City Americans of Kennewick, Washington, were stunned when director of hockey operations Bill LaForge, on the job for 10 days, blasted the team. "He wasn't even our coach and he came in and started swearing at us and bossing us around," complained goalie Olaf Kolzig. The Americans countered by going on strike, forcing cancellation of their next game. LaForge was quickly transferred to a new position within the organization.

Some of My Personal Favourites NINE

As the world's most famous hockey puck, I pride myself in always playing fair. I never slide across the goal line just to help a poor rookie score his first goal. He's got to earn it. And I never jump off the stick of a bruiser who's belted me around and make him look bad, just because I don't like his attitude.

For the most part, I hope everyone playing hockey does well. But while I'm known to be impartial, I must admit I've had some favourite players, referees, and coaches over the years.

● **Defenceman Doug Harvey,** after 14 seasons with the Montreal Canadiens, was traded to the New York Rangers in 1961. As playing coach in New York, he captured the Norris Trophy as the NHL's top rearguard, becoming the first coach to win a player trophy and the first man to win back-to-back Norris Trophies with two different teams.

● **Defenceman Bill Gadsby** played 20 seasons in the NHL without ever winning the Stanley Cup. But he was lucky to play even a single game. In 1939, when he was 12 years old, his mother took him on a trip to England to visit relatives. While they were there, war broke out with Germany and the Gadsbys booked passage back to North

America on the *Athenia*. But a German torpedo sank the ship, and hundreds of passengers were left floating in life-boats in the North Atlantic, Gadsby and his mother among them. Eventually, most were rescued and brought back to England. Days later, aboard the *Mauretania*, they arrived safely in New York.

● **Bobby Bauer,** a member of Boston's famous Kraut Line, returned to the NHL after a five-year absence for one final celebrated contest. Bauer joined his old linemates,

Milt Schmidt and Woody Dumart, for a final game together on March 18, 1952, the night their numbers were retired by the Boston Bruins. Early in the game, Schmidt scored his 200th career goal with Bauer and Dumart assisting. The Boston faithful roared like they hadn't in years. Bobby Bauer scored a goal and an assist in his final NHL game.

● **It took 22 seasons** and 214 playoff games before Colorado Avalanche defenceman Ray Bourque was able to lift the Stanley Cup over his head. He said to me, "Pete, I didn't think this day would ever come." Bourque's memorable day came on June 9, 2001, in Denver when the Colorado Rockies captured the Stanley Cup with a 3–1 defeat of the New Jersey Devils in game seven. Bourque, the top-scoring defenceman of all time, spent all but the last season of his Hall of Fame career as a Boston Bruin.

● **On October 20, 1993,** Wayne Gretzky scored a goal and added two assists in a game featuring two Gretzkys. Wayne played against his brother Brent, 21, who was appearing in his second NHL game. Brent Gretzky played in 13 NHL games for Tampa Bay over two seasons and scored one goal—893 fewer than his older brother. Most people aren't aware that Wayne's kid brother enjoyed a stint in the NHL.

● **Did you know** that Brett Hull and his father, Bobby, both won the Hart Trophy as the NHL's MVP? What I can't figure out is why so many teams ignored Brett when he was draftable. Didn't they notice the 52 goals he scored one season at the University of Minnesota? The Calgary Flames finally took him in the sixth round, 117th overall, and then traded him to St. Louis when they didn't see his scoring potential. In St. Louis, he scored 86 goals one year and won the Hart Trophy. Later, he won a Stanley Cup with the Dallas Stars and another with the Detroit Red Wings before he retired with 741 goals, 131 more than his famous father. But don't forget Bobby Hull scored 303 goals in the WHA, a rival league. Brett joined his dad in the Hockey Hall of Fame in November 2009.

● **Detroit's Steve Yzerman** was the longest-serving team captain in all of professional major sports history. He was given the "C" in 1986 at age 21, and in the next two decades he led Detroit to three Stanley Cups. He scored 692 career goals, sixth among career goal-scoring leaders, and was inducted into the Hockey Hall of Fame in 2009. But get this! When *The Hockey News* listed the 50 all-time greatest players, Yzerman was not listed. Only when the list was expanded to 100 did his name appear—in the 78th spot.

Man, was he overlooked and underrated!

● **When he was** in the fourth grade, Jonathan Cheechoo wrote an essay about his future. He predicted he'd play for the San Jose Sharks in the NHL one day. He grew up, became a professional hockey player, and was signed by the Sharks. How about that for making a dream come true? "I thought my essay was pretty good," he recalls "but I only got a C+ from my teacher." Cheechoo, the first member of the Moose Cree Nation to play in the NHL, scored 56 goals in 2005–06 to win the Maurice Richard Trophy as the league's top goal scorer. But he's struggled since then. Traded to Ottawa, he scored a mere five goals in 61 games in 2009–10 and finished the season in Binghamton of the AHL. What a comedown!

● **While growing up** in Alberta, Nigerian-born Jarome Iginla played catcher on the Canadian junior baseball team. He was a goaltender during his first two years of organized hockey. With the Calgary Flames in 2002, he captured the Art Ross Trophy as leading scorer in the NHL with 96 points. He added the Maurice Richard Trophy for most goals with 52.

Jarome's father, Adekule Iginla, changed his first name to Elvis when people had trouble pronouncing Adekule. Jarome can sing, too. Perhaps I'll ask him to sing the national anthem before a Calgary game.

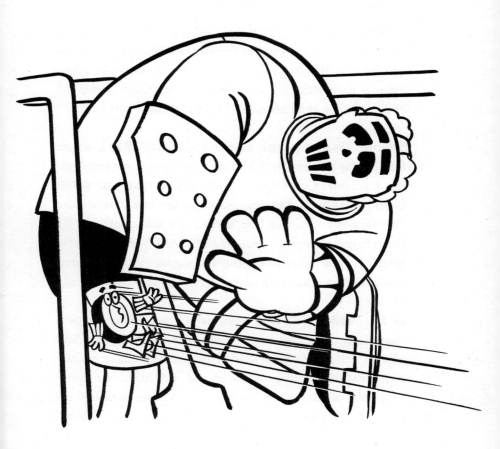

● **The Washington Capitals'** Alexander Ovechkin inherited much of his athletic talent from his mother, Tatiana. She won Olympic gold medals in 1976 and 1980 while starring for the Soviet national basketball team. Ovechkin recently signed a contract extension, which will net him $124 million over 13 years, $9 million per season for the first six years and $10 million per season for the following seven years.

You know what? I think he can now afford to buy a new front tooth and a razor. He looks like he doesn't shave often, and he has a gap between his teeth.

● **Let's hear it** for Chris Pronger! A total of nine penalty shots have been awarded in Stanley Cup finals history, but only one of the free shots has been successful. In 2006, Pronger, then with the Edmonton Oilers, scored on Cam Ward of the Carolina Hurricanes. And Pronger is a defenceman.

● **Scott Niedermayer,** captain of Canada's 2010 Olympic team, is the only player in history to win every major award: the Memorial Cup, World Junior Championships, World Championships, Olympics, Stanley Cup, and World Cup. This four-time Stanley Cup winner has also captured the Conn Smythe Trophy as playoff MVP (2007) and the James Norris Trophy as the NHL's top defenceman (2004). Scotty, you've had an amazing career. Peter Puck is proud of you.

● **In 1993–94,** Teemu Selanne of the Winnipeg Jets shattered rookie scoring records with 76 goals and 132 points. No rookie since has come close to those marks. Neither has Selanne, although he did have two more 50-plus-goal seasons and he's compiled more than 600 career goals. What's more, at the 2010 Olympic Games, competing for Finland, Selanne became the all-time Olympic-points-scoring champion. So I say, let's put him in the Hockey Hall of Fame someday soon—next to the only other Finn inducted, Jari Kurri.

⬤ **Did you know** that 10 members of Buffalo goalie Ryan Miller's family have played college hockey for the Michigan State Spartans? Ryan's grandfather, father, uncle, five cousins, and his younger brother, Drew, all suited up for Michigan State.

⬤ **In 1985,** the Red Wings made U.S. college player Adam Oates the richest rookie in NHL history. The Rensselaer Polytechnic Institute grad, a two-time All American, signed a four-year contract for $1.1 million. A few days later, the Red Wings signed a second college player, Ray Staszak of the University of Illinois at Chicago, to a sweeter deal— $1.3 million. Oates played 19 years with seven different clubs and collected over 1,000 points. Staszak's career consisted of four games for Detroit. He assisted on one goal.

⬤ **The Buffalo Sabres** have been participating in the NHL's annual draft since 1970, and their first choice remains their best. Gilbert Perreault, selected number one in 1970, went on to set team records for games played (1191), goals (512), assists (814), and total points (1326). Perreault was inducted into the Hockey Hall of Fame in 1990.

⬤ **In the spring** of 1973, the New York Rangers eliminated the Boston Bruins from the Stanley Cup playoffs. During the series, Bruins star Phil Esposito was hospitalized in Boston with a leg injury. But when the Bruins held a post-season party, they decided that Esposito must attend, bad leg and all. They decided to kidnap their leader—for just a few hours.

While some of the Bruins distracted the nurses on duty, others wheeled Esposito, still in his hospital bed, down an elevator and out a side exit. Somehow, a metal railing was broken during the escape. The Bruins guided the hospital bed and its famous patient down the avenue while drivers beeped their horns and moved out of the way. Led by Wayne Cashman and Bobby Orr, the players wheeled Esposito around a corner to a restaurant.

When the Bruins were partied out, they wheeled Esposito back to the hospital, where officials confronted them. One of them presented the Bruins with an invoice for "damages to hospital property."

Cashman and Orr took care of the situation. While Espo slept, his mates slipped the invoice into his pyjama pocket.

● **The U.S hockey team's** gold medal victory at the 1980 Winter Olympics at Lake Placid, New York, was a triumph of such magnitude that all of North America got caught up in it. And I was thrilled to be there. When it was over, they called it the Miracle on Main Street.

The USSR had won every gold medal at the Olympics for the past 16.

And the Soviets toyed with the Americans in a pre-tournament game, whipping them 11–3.

When the young Americans—average age 20—met the defending champs in the tournament's biggest game, they kept pace with their highly touted opponents. The game was tied 3–3 in the third period. Then U.S. team captain Mike Eruzione slapped a high, hard shot over goalie Vladimir Myshkin's glove and the red light flashed. United States 4, Soviets 3. There was an incredible explosion of noise in the arena on Main Street. Fans roared their approval and waved American flags. Coach Herb Brooks' players held on to win the game, triggering a wild celebration on the ice at the finish. Only Helmuts Balderis of the Soviet team skated over to congratulate the winners. He shook hands with coach Brooks while Soviet coach Viktor Tikhonov glowered at Balderis.

Man, those teams disliked each other.

Two days later, the Americans had to win again, this time against Finland, if they were to capture the gold. The Finns led 2–1 midway through the game. Coach Brooks urged his charges to rally, and they did, winning the match 4–2. The post-game celebration seemed to go on forever.

It's been more than 30 years since that memorable moment on Main Street. But who can ever forget it? The young Americans basked in Olympic glory.

● **Eric Lindros** was drafted first overall by the Quebec Nordiques in 1991, but he refused to play for the team. A year later, he was traded to the Philadelphia Flyers for goalie Ron Hextall, defencemen Steve Duchesne and Kerry Huffman, forwards Mike Ricci and Chris Simon, prospect Peter Forsberg, a 1993 draft pick, and $15 million. Forsberg alone made up for the loss of Lindros. Each played in over 700 games. Forsberg amassed 885 points to Lindros's 865.

● **Joey Mullen** overcame amazing odds to become a star in the NHL. He grew up in Hell's Kitchen in New York, a tough neighbourhood. For years, he played on rollerblades with a roll of electrical tape for a puck. Luckily, his father worked at Madison Square Garden, where Mullen and his brother, Brian, were able to get some ice time. Eventually, both made it to the NHL, but Joey excelled. He played on three Stanley Cup teams, once with Calgary and twice with Pittsburgh, and was the first American-born player to score 500 goals. He was also the first to collect 1,000 points. Mullen was inducted into the Hockey Hall of Fame in 2000. Atta boy, Joey!

● **Mark "Moose" Messier** played 25 seasons in the NHL over four decades. He holds the record for the most regular season and playoff games played with 1,992. Messier won five Stanley Cups with the Edmonton Oilers and a sixth with the New York Rangers in 1994. When the Rangers retired his jersey number 11 on January 12, 2006, several front row seats to the event were sold for $30,000. Since August 16, 2009, Messier has served as special assistant to Rangers general manager Glen Sather.

● **Paul Provost,** an Ottawa boy, figured he was too small for NHL play, so he accepted a position as player-coach of a team in France. Playing against a touring Russian team one night on an outdoor rink, a blizzard dumped several inches of snow on the ice. "I couldn't see the puck," Provost confessed later, "but it hit my foot and jumped up into my glove. I skated in behind the Russian net and dropped it in behind their netminder. The goal judge and the referee spotted it there and signalled a goal. I knew what had happened, but nobody else did. I didn't say a word and I got credit for the goal that tied the game."

● **Ever heard** of a scoring star named Dong Song? You may not believe this, but *The Hockey News* will confirm it. In 1998, during the Asia-Oceania junior championships, South Korea won a hockey game by a score of 92–0. South Korea's star player, Donghwan Song, scored 10 hat tricks in the game and was on his way to an 11th when time ran out. He finished with 31 goals and 5 assists for 36 points. It was the largest score and the most one-sided game in hockey history.

● **In January 2007,** Teemu Selanne of the Anaheim Ducks learned that a friend was seriously ill with cancer and the outlook was not good. Selanne promised his friend that he'd score a hat trick for him and give him the puck as a souvenir. Selanne wondered how he could keep such a promise, as he had not scored a hat trick in six seasons. But on the following day, against the Dallas Stars, Sellane potted three goals and was able to retrieve the puck for his friend.

● **Ilya Kovalchuk** of the New Jersey Devils was the first Russian hockey player to be drafted first overall in the 2001 NHL Entry Draft. Before being traded to New Jersey in 2010, he starred with the Atlanta Thrashers. In the final year of his contract with the Thrashers, he reportedly turned down a 12-year, $101-million pact to stay in Georgia.

● **Bobby and Brett Hull** are the only father and son combo to score more than 50 goals in a season and more than 600 career NHL goals. They are also the only father and son tandem to win the Hart Trophy and Lady Byng Trophy. Bobby and Brett are the only father and son combination in any professional sport to both have their numbers retired. Bobby's number 9 was retired by the Chicago Black Hawks and Winnipeg Jets (now Phoenix Coyotes), and Brett's number 16 was retired by the St. Louis Blues. In 2005, while playing for the Coyotes, Brett donned his father's retired number 9 for the last five games of his career.

● **On Saturday,** January 12, 1985, the Canadiens' all-time "dream team" was honoured in a special ceremony at the Montreal Forum. The event coincided with the team's 75th anniversary.

More than 20,000 ballots were tabulated to name the members of the team. The fans selected:

- Goalie Jacques Plante, who played on five straight Stanley Cup winners from 1956 to 1960 and captured six Vezina Trophies.
- Defenceman Doug Harvey, nine times an NHL All-Star.
- Defenceman Larry Robinson, twice a winner of the Norris Trophy.
- Centre Jean Béliveau, an extraordinary playmaker and scorer for 18 seasons.
- Left winger Dickie Moore, a fierce competitor and two-time NHL scoring champion in the late 1950s.
- Right winger Maurice Richard, who scored 544 regular season goals and was the first NHL player to score 50 goals in 50 games.
- Toe Blake, who guided the Habs to eight Stanley Cups in 13 seasons and was named coach of the dream team.

The second team:

- Goalie Ken Dryden
- Defenceman Serge Savard
- Defenceman J. C. Tremblay
- Centre Henri Richard
- Left winger Toe Blake
- Right winger Guy Lafleur
- Coach Scotty Bowman

Special guest Aurel Joliat, then 83 and the oldest living former Hab, was honoured, as was Bob Gainey, then captain and left winger for the Canadiens.

⬤ **Frank "King" Clancy** sparked the Leafs to a Stanley Cup triumph in 1932. He retired during the 1936–37 season and coached the Montreal Maroons the following season. Then he turned to refereeing and became one of the most respected officials in the game. He coached the Leafs from 1953 to 1956 and served the club after that as assistant general manager and "vice-president in charge of nothing," to borrow his own job description.

One day I heard him tell some reporters about a "night" the Leafs held for him at Maple Leaf Gardens:

Boys, whenever I think back to March 17, 1934, and recall how the Leafs honoured me with a "night" on St. Patrick's Day, I get a lump in my throat. Can you believe they talked me into getting dressed in a green uniform with a big white shamrock stitched on the back? They had me wear a long white beard and somebody placed a crown on my head. A huge crowd filled the Gardens that night to see the shenanigans and a nasty game that followed against the New York Rangers.

The Rangers were good sports and joined in the fun. Their big defenceman, Ching Johnson, hauled a huge float onto the ice in the shape of a potato. The crowd was sure I was inside the float. But they were fooled when it opened up and some junior B players from St. Mikes flew out.

Then a lot of other floats appeared and I wasn't in any of those either. One of my teammates, Ken

Doraty, came out of a large pipe and Harold Cotton popped out of a huge top hat. Our trainer, Tim Daly, was hidden in a big bottle of ginger ale and goalie George Hainsworth emerged from inside a big boot. Red Horner, the team tough guy, stepped out of a giant boxing glove, which was appropriate, and Gentleman Joe Primeau came out of a harp, of all things.

When a big shamrock showed up, the crowd roared because they thought I was inside it. But Bill Cook, a great Ranger star, stepped out and took a bow.

When my turn finally came, the lights in the building were dimmed. Then, wearing my royal robes, my crown, and my scraggly beard, I was ushered in on a makeshift throne, pulled along the ice by my pal Hap Day. When the float reached centre ice, I stepped down. Then everything went black because either Charlie Conacher or Day threw a mittful of chimney soot in my face. They showed no respect for royalty at all. So when the lights came up, I stood there looking like a king all right, except that my face was pitch black. It took me two or three days of hard scrubbing to get the darn stuff off.

But it turned out to be a fantastic night. They gave me a grandfather clock and a silver tea service for my wife. I think I was the first Leaf player ever to be given a "night" and it was one of the greatest things that ever happened to me in sports.

Anyway, I wore my green uniform for the first period of the game that followed. After the first period, Lester Patrick, the Ranger coach, told me I'd better change back to a blue shirt because the green sweater with the shamrock on back was confusing to the other players.

Remember the WHA? **TEN**

Most of my young readers won't remember the World Hockey Association. It was rival league to the NHL—and a thorn in the established league's side—that operated from 1972 to 1979.

The new league attracted some of the best players because it paid higher salaries and doled out long-term contracts.

Here are some fascinating facts about the league that, until it merged with the NHL in 1979, gave NHL team owners plenty of costly headaches.

● **In the new league's** first season, 67 players jumped from the NHL to the WHA. Most did not return until the NHL swallowed up four of the WHA franchises in 1979.

● **Chicago Black Hawks** superstar Bobby Hull gave the WHA instant credibility in 1972 when he signed a 10-year, $2.75-million contract to play for the Winnipeg Jets. It was a record contract at the time. All the other WHA owners chipped in to meet Hull's asking price.

● **The WHA was introduced** in 1971 with 10 teams agreeing to pay $25,000 for a franchise.

⬤ **Star goaltender** Bernie Parent of the Leafs was one of the first to jump leagues. He signed with the Miami Screaming Eagles, a team that never got off the ground. Later, it surfaced as the Philadelphia Blazers.

⬤ **Opening night** in Philadelphia turned out to be a nightmare for the hometown Blazers and former Boston Bruin star Derek Sanderson. The ice surface in the refurbished Convention Hall was deemed unsafe and unplayable when the Zamboni fell through the ice up to its axles. When Sanderson, who'd just signed a $2-million dollar contract with the Blazers, took the microphone at centre ice and told the crowd the game was cancelled, they threw hundreds of souvenir pucks at him. Sanderson was injured

early in the new season and played only a handful of games for the Blazers. Someone figured the former star was making $2,300 per day, "and he doesn't even have to put on his skates." The Blazers bought out his contract at the end of the season, leaving him with a reported million dollars.

● **The WHA** loaded up with European players. The Winnipeg Jets brought in Scandinavian players and soared to the top of the league. Swedish sensations Anders Hedberg and Ulf Nilsson formed a line with Bobby Hull that was magical to watch.

● **The Los Angeles Sharks** opened their first season at home on Friday the 13th against Houston. The pucks hadn't been frozen before the game and bounced around like rubber balls. And when the Zamboni driver flooded the ice at the intermission, black liquid oozed out from under the machine and covered a large patch of ice.

● **Goalie Bernie Parent** enjoyed a fine season with the Blazers in 1972–73, but he walked out on his team in the playoffs. Parent claimed the Blazers had failed to deposit the final $100,000 of his $750,000 contract and he refused to play. Without Parent, the Blazers lost four straight play-off games and their season was over. Parent jumped back to the NHL the following year and won back-to-back Stanley Cups with the Philadelphia Flyers—plus two Conn Smythe Trophies.

● **Tony McKegney** got a shock prior to the 1978 season. The 20-year-old was told he would not be offered a contract to play with the Birmingham Bulls of the WHA because his asking price was too high—and because certain ticket holders to Bulls games were bothered because McKegney was black.

● **In 1978,** Nelson Skalbania, owner of the Indianapolis club in the WHA, signed 17-year-old Wayne Gretzky to a seven-year personal services contract estimated at $1.7 million. Gretzky still had three years of junior eligibility remaining.

● **The New England Whalers** won the first league title and would have paraded the gleaming Avco Trophy around the ice in celebration. But there was no Avco Trophy. It hadn't been created yet.

● **The Toronto Toros,** formerly the Ottawa Nationals, played at Maple Leaf Gardens. Harold Ballard, the crusty owner of the building, who was in jail at the time, charged the Toros $15,000 per game. He demanded another $3,500 per game for the use of additional lighting and forced the Toros to build their own dressing room at a cost of $50,000. The Toros soon packed up and moved to Birmingham, Alabama.

● **Many hockey legends** got their start in the WHA, including Wayne Gretzky and Mark Messier, who played as teenagers for the Indianapolis Racers. Messier also played for Cincinnati but received little attention. He played in 52 WHA games and scored just one goal.

● **John Tonelli** jumped from junior hockey with the Marlboros to play with Houston in the WHA. On his first shift, he played on a line with Gordie and Mark Howe. "We came back to the bench after the shift. I'm 18 years old and very nervous. Suddenly Gordie leans toward me and wipes his dripping nose all over my sweater. I did not say one word. I just kept looking at the play. But looking back, I always laugh about it. It was so . . . so Gordie Howe. His snot all over my sleeve."

⬤ **In 1973–74,** Terry Slater, general manager of the WHA's Los Angeles Sharks, was not happy when coach Ted McCaskill suggested a few player changes. The first player he wanted to get rid of was Slater's brother. It wasn't long before Slater was coaching and McCaskill was back playing again.

⬤ **In March 1974,** head referee Bill Friday was furious when he learned that the Chicago Cougars had used a suspended player, Connie Forey, in a game against Quebec. Forey had been suspended by the league for slugging and injuring referee Malcolm Ashford. "If I'd known he was out there, it would have been my gear off or his," Friday proclaimed. Forey's suspension was for all of the 1973–74 season. In addition, he was ordered to pay Ashford $10,000 in damages. After his lone game with the Cougars, Forey was banished from further play in the WHA.

⬤ **The WHA's** Minnesota Fighting Saints sought playing talent in the most unlikely places. They offered a tryout to Fern Tessier, just out of prison in Quebec after serving an 11-year stretch for robbery. Fern the felon wasn't good enough to become a Saint.

⬤ **Minnesota coach** Harry Neale looked down his bench during a game one night and witnessed an amazing sight. Two of his Fighting Saints were duking it out with each other. When the referee skated over, Neale quipped, "You can't give them penalties. They're both on the same team."

● **In Chicago,** for the first time in hockey history, professional players became part owners of a team. WHA players Pat Stapleton, Dave Dryden, and Ralph Backstrom became principal investors in their own team, the Chicago Cougars.

● **In 1974–75,** Bobby Hull broke the major professional league record for goals when he tallied 77 for the Winnipeg Jets. The Jets' Hull-Nilsson-Hedberg line netted 363 points, 27 more than the previous pro record set by Boston's line of Esposito, Cashman, and Hodge. Hedberg, with 53 goals, was the top rookie in the WHA.

● **In the 1975–76** WHA playoffs, violence erupted in a series between Quebec and Calgary. Calgary's Rick Jodzio charged Quebec's Marc Tardif, hitting the left winger so hard he was rushed to hospital with a concussion. Criminal charges were laid against Jodzio, who was suspended by the WHA "possibly for all time." It triggered the wildest donnybrook in the brief history of the league. At least 20 Quebec policemen were on the ice trying to restore order. Ben Hatskin, the league's chief executive officer, suspended Jodzio for the rest of the series and "possibly for all time" and suspended Calgary coach Joe Crozier for the rest of the playoff series between the two clubs. He also fined the teams $25,000 each for failing to control their players in the most violent battle in the history of the WHA.

● **Bobby Hull** made no bones about how he felt. Talking about the state of hockey, he said, "I may retire at the end of the season. The game isn't much fun anymore. It's getting to be a disaster. The idiot owners, the incompetent coaches, the inept players are dragging the game into the mud. They're destroying it with all the senseless violence."

● **In 1978,** the Philadelphia Flyers purchased forward Ken Linesman from the WHA's Birmingham Bulls for a reported $500,000.

● **The WHA tried** all manner of stunts and promotions to attract the fans. When André Lacroix went to Philadelphia, he agreed to let them lock him in a bank vault for several days as a publicity stunt.

● **The Cincinnati Stingers** had a mascot that skated around the ice dressed like a bee. Before a game one night, an opposing player smashed into the bee and the little mascot crumpled to the ice like he'd been hit by a huge fly swatter. There was a gasp of disbelief from the crowd and a lot of laughter from the rival bench when that happened.

● **The Toronto Toros** brought daredevil Evel Knievel to Maple Leaf Gardens to compete in a penalty shot shootout against goalie Les Binkley. There was a lot of hoopla and a $20,000 prize at stake. Knievel had to score on 50 per cent of his shots to collect the prize—a tough task for someone who hadn't been on skates in years. Knievel fooled everybody by scoring on two out of four shots and skating off with the 20 grand. And he did it with a hangover. Jim Dorey, a Toro at the time, was told to escort the famous daredevil on a pub crawl. The idea was to get Knievel so inebriated he'd never be able to score a goal the following day. So Dorey and Knievel stayed out all night and got blasted—on owner Johnny Basset's credit card. Dorey told me, "Knievel drank me under the table, and while I nursed the biggest hangover in my life the following day, Knievel was up bright and early and eager to test goalie Les Binkley with his shots. I couldn't believe my eyes when he scored on two of them and grabbed the 20 grand."

● **Wayne Gretzky,** age 17, was signed by Nelson Skalbania for his Indianapolis club. He even let Wayne write out the contract himself—in longhand—during an airplane flight. What a marvellous coup that was, signing Gretzky. At least two NHL scouts went down to see Gretzky play in the WHA, and they both agreed that he'd never make the NHL. He was too frail, too skinny, and not at all tough enough to stand the rough going. If you see those fellows in a roomful of scouts today, they'll be the ones with the red faces.

● **The WHA** lasted less than a decade, but it caused the NHL a multitude of headaches. And it was a fountain for those of us who thirst for bizarre hockey stories.

About the Game Officials

Fans who watch a hockey game seldom notice the game officials—the two referees and two linesmen. That means they're doing a solid job. Game officials love to go unnoticed. It's when controversial calls are made, when a referee misses an obvious penalty, when a linesman gets in the way of the puck carrier or blows an offside call at the blue line, that fans go wild.

Since hockey's earliest days, game officials have been roasted by fans and sometimes assaulted by players, team managers, and coaches. It's not a job that just anybody can do.

● **In 1910,** Bad Joe Hall of the Montreal Shamrocks attacked game official Rod Kennedy, who was working a game in Renfrew. Hall beat Kennedy with his fists and ripped Kennedy's new suit apart. Hall was fined $100 but refused to pay. Ultimately, the Shamrocks paid the fine, plus $27 to cover the cost of Kennedy's suit.

● **It wasn't until 1913** that referees began dropping the puck on faceoffs. Until then, the referee placed the puck between the two centres and shouted, "Play!"

● **Referees and linesmen** learn to develop thick skins and tune out verbal abuse. They chuckle over some of the barbs and taunts they've heard. As an NHL referee, King Clancy worked a game in New York one night in the forties. Just before the opening faceoff, there was a 21-gun salute for some reason or other. After the gunfire ended, a loudmouth fan shouted, "Now that's over with, you can shoot Clancy!"

Clancy leaped up on the boards in Chicago one night, and a lady at rinkside moved in and stuck him in the rear with a hatpin. He refused to continue until she was removed from the arena.

● **In 1924,** little Leo Dandurand refereed a game in Montreal between the Canadiens and the Wanderers. Even though the Canadiens won 6–5 in overtime, Canadiens manager George Kennedy was furious with Dandurand. He marched across the ice and attacked him with both fists. Then he followed him to the officials' dressing room, where he insulted him in the worst manner, calling him vile names.

● **When Eddie Shore** owned the Springfield Indians in the AHL in the 1960s, he had little tolerance for game officials. If a referee made a glaring mistake, he might find himself locked in or out of the officials' dressing room. Shore had the key to the padlock on the door. If Shore felt the official was truly inept, he was apt to denounce the poor man over the public address system in the arena.

● **On December 29, 1955,** in a game between Montreal and Toronto, the game officials wore new vertically striped black and white jerseys for the first time.

Have you noticed how smartly dressed the on-ice officials look today? They are traditionally clad in a black hockey helmet, black trousers, a black and white striped shirt, and black polished skates with white laces. They wear standard hockey skates and carry a whistle, which they use often to stop play. They communicate with players, coaches, and off-ice officials, both verbally and with hand signals. For many years, and currently in most minor and amateur leagues, officials wore their last names on the back of their jerseys for identification. Since 1994, however, NHL officials have worn numbers on their shirts, a procedure that has been adopted by other leagues.

In the early days of hockey, the referees would be clad in

a vest and tie along with knee-length pants and stockings, and they carried a bell, not a whistle. In those days, penalties were assessed more on common sense rather than by following strict rules, and the referee would decide what was allowed and not, as well as the length of the penalties.

Until penalty boxes were invented—and nobody seems to know when that was—penalized players were told to sit on the low boards at rinkside. After a set time, the referee would wave them back into the game.

● **Let's examine** the duties of modern-day referees, linesmen, and other game officials.

- A referee is responsible for the general supervision of the game, and he can be identified by his red or orange armbands. Under most officiating systems, he is the only official with the authority to assess penalties for violations of the rules; however, the linesmen can also call a variety of penalties, such as too many players on the ice, and major penalties in a case where the referee was unable to identify it. The referee also conducts the opening faceoff in each period and faceoffs at centre after a goal is scored.
- Linesmen are primarily responsible for watching for violations involving the centre line and the blue line. Such infractions include icing and offside infractions. Linesmen also conduct most faceoffs and are expected to break up scuffles, fights, and other altercations that occur during the game. Some leagues allow linesmen to call penalties, such as too many players on the ice, while others allow them only to report the infraction to the referee.

⚫ **Off-ice officials,** with the exception of the video goal judge in professional leagues, have less importance when it comes to the outcome of the game.

- The goal judge determines whether a player has scored a goal by watching to see if the puck has crossed the goal line completely. The goal judge turns on a red light behind the goal to signal that a goal has just been scored. The red light, and the green light, which is mounted next to it, are hooked up to the game clock. The green light signals the end of each period and the red light cannot come on when the game clock reads 00:00.

  Goal judges were first introduced around 1877 in Montreal and were initially called umpires. They stood out on the ice behind the goal net and signalled a score by waving a hankie in the air. Often they were chosen from the crowd, spectators who volunteered to take on the job—without pay.

  They had to be nimble to avoid collisions with players chasing pucks in behind the net.
- The video goal judge is relatively new to hockey. His job is to review disputed goals. As the referee doesn't have access to television monitors, the video goal judge's decision in disputed goals is taken as final. In the NHL, goals may only be reviewed in the following situations: puck crossing the goal line completely and before time expired, puck in the net prior to goal frame being dislodged, puck being directed into the net by hand or foot, puck deflected into the net off an official, and puck deflected into the goal by a high stick—stick above the goal—by an attacking player. All NHL goals are subject to review, and although most arenas have a video goal judge, reviewers in the "War Room" at the

NHL office in Toronto often make the final decision.

- The scorer keeps the official record of the game. He is responsible for obtaining a list of eligible players from both teams before the start of the game. He awards points for goals and assists, and his decision in this regard is final. The scorer typically sits in an elevated position away from the edge of the rink.
- The penalty timekeeper records the penalties imposed by the referee. He is responsible for ensuring that the correct penalty times are posted on the score clock and that players leave the penalty box at the appropriate times.
- The game timekeeper is responsible for stopping and starting the game clock.
- The statistician records all required data concerning individual and team performances.

● **The four major league** sports have no trouble finding applicants for jobs as umpires and referees. The salaries are thought to be well worth the aggravation that comes with the territory.

Major League Baseball pays umpires anywhere from US$100,000 to $280,000 for the 162-game season, in addition to the sum of more than $50,000 per season for expenses. This does not include the cost of first-class air travel, which is provided. The lucky ones who get to call the games in the post-season make somewhere in the ballpark of $20,000, excluding expenses.

National Basketball Association referees earn anywhere from $90,000 to $225,000 per season.

Incidentally, no rookie officials in any of the other major sports make more than those in the NHL, where starters earn $115,000 a year. After a 15-year career, an NHL referee may garner an annual salary upwards of $220,000.

The National Football League pays referees anywhere from $25,000 to $70,000 per season, but they work a maximum of 16 games. They also get a one-week break between assignments.

● **And where are the** women officials? There are none in the NHL. Referees in the Women's National Basketball Association earn about $500 per game for a 32-game season, or a maximum of $16,000 annually.

● **One of my favourite** NHL officials was Don Koharski, who retired in 2009 at age 53 after a 32-year NHL career.

Koharski was involved in an infamous incident during a 1988 playoff series between the New Jersey Devils and Boston Bruins. Jim Schoenfeld, then coach of the Devils, waited for him in the Meadowlands Arena hallway after the Devils lost 6–1 in game three. He called Koharski a "fat pig" and screamed at him and told him to "have another dough-nut." Koharski claims he doesn't even eat doughnuts. The incident triggered a one-game walkout by the league's referees when a court injunction allowed Schoenfeld to coach the next game despite the NHL's punishment of a one-game suspension. Wasn't it odd that the judge who handled the injunction happened to be a big Devils' fan? Schoenfeld apologized to Koharski long ago, and the two have maintained a friendly relationship since.

Highlights of Koharski's career include his first Stanley Cup final and working the 1987 Canada Cup final between Canada and the Soviet Union, in which the Russians asked for him to be the referee.

● **A popular former** NHL linesman passed away on November 19, 1987. George Hayes was 67. Hayes had worked 1,549 games between 1946 and 1955 before being suspended by NHL president Clarence Campbell for refusing to take an eye examination. Hayes' flippant response was to say he didn't need an eye exam because he took one every night reading the labels on whiskey bottles. Hayes was also known to make his own sandwiches, which he took on road trips. By mistake, he confused a can of tuna fish with a can of dog food before leaving on a trip to Detroit. When he took to the ice, Gordie Howe and some of the Red Wings started barking at him.

⬤**For the 1956–57** season, game officials allowed a player serving a minor penalty to return to the ice after a goal was scored by the opposing team—a power play goal. Until then, a player served his full time in the box. The rule was intended to thwart the Montreal Canadiens' great power play, which sometimes clicked for two or three goals while playing with a man advantage.

Hockey Here and There TWELVE

All kinds of people get involved with hockey: multi-millionaires and crooked agents, players who are as tall as basketball stars and others as tiny as jockeys, coaches who've never played and players who can't coach. Goons who've been suspended for life, teams that will play for 72 straight hours, and goalies who've worn boxing gloves. Read on!

⬤ **When the Original Six** NHL teams invited six new franchises to the NHL family in 1967, hockey changed dramatically.

Before NHL expansion, teams played each other 14 times per season and the rivalries were fierce. Toronto and Montreal were the bitterest foes. Future Hall of Famers were all over the ice when these clubs clashed. Béliveau, the Richards, Harvey, Plante, Geoffrion, and other brilliant Habs versus Bower, Horton, Stanley, Armstrong, Keon, Kelly, and similarly gifted Leafs.

No helmets. No names on the jerseys. No player agents. No million-dollar salaries. No thought of bringing players over from Europe or scouting and recruiting college players. Those fellows were lowly amateurs. There was no talk then of expansion to distant cities like Los Angeles or even Vancouver. And no inkling of a rival league, the WHA, on the far horizon.

179

⬤ **Saturday night** was hockey night. It was a tradition that began with radio in the thirties. Then, from 1952 on, all across Canada families gathered in their living rooms to watch the games on black and white TV. And televised games couldn't be seen until the first period was over. Youngsters were seldom allowed to watch a complete game before being ordered off to bed. Wives made trips to the kitchen to gossip with other wives and prepare snacks for the male viewers.

⬤ **Many of the** telecast crew—Foster and Bill Hewitt, Jack Dennett, Ward Cornell, Danny Gallivan, and Dick Irvin—quickly became household names, as familiar as the powder blue jackets they wore on television. Foster's three star selections were as eagerly awaited as the national news, and he was accused of picking "the two goalies and Keon" far too often.

⬤ **In the 1970s,** right winger Helmut Balderis was the best player in Latvia and one of the top stars in the Soviet league. After scoring 333 career goals, in 1985 he retired to coach in Japan. In 1989, after a long absence from the game as a player, at age 36 he became the oldest player ever drafted by an NHL club as a rookie with the Minnesota North Stars. At 37, he became the oldest player to score his first NHL goal. Sadly, his skills had faded. Balderis scored three goals in 26 games for the North Stars and was released.

⬤ **Did you know** that Detroit Red Wing owner Mike Ilitch was once a promising baseball player? But his call to the majors never came, so he became a door-to-door sales-man. He earned enough money selling pots and pans to open a pizza restaurant called Little Caesar's in 1959. The restaurant flourished and he opened several more. In 1982, he was wealthy enough to purchase the struggling Detroit Red Wings for a mere $8 million, and soon his team was one of the most successful in the NHL. In 2009, Forbes listed the Red Wings' worth at $337 million.

● **Don Murdoch,** the New York Rangers' number one pick in the 1976 Entry Draft, made a spectacular debut in the NHL, scoring eight goals in his first three games. Five of the goals came in one game to tie a rookie record. By mid-season, he had 32 goals and might have set a record for goals by a first-year player if injuries hadn't sidelined him. Then Murdoch fell in with the wrong crowd in Manhattan. Drinking and drugs became a problem. He was caught smuggling cocaine into Canada and was suspended for a year. He never recaptured the form that had made him a rookie sensation. After stops in Detroit and Edmonton, he was shunted to the minors.

● **Vincent Damphousse** is the only player in NHL history to lead three different teams in scoring in consecutive seasons. In 1990–91, Damphousse led the Toronto Maple Leafs with 73 points. The following season, traded to Edmonton, he collected a team high 89 points. Another trade sent him to Montreal, where he topped all his teammates with 97 points.

I know, I know. Some of you wiseacres will say that Lanny McDonald led Toronto, Colorado, and Calgary in scoring—and he did. But not in consecutive seasons.

● **When tough guys** John Brophy and Don Perry teamed up on defence for the Long Island Ducks in the old Eastern Hockey League, they were masters of intimidation. Playing at home against the New Haven Blades one night, they clobbered two or three of the visitors on their very first shift. That was enough. The Blades fled the ice, put on their street clothes and went home. The game lasted all of 80 seconds.

● **During the 1982–83** season, a bizarre trade took place in the Western Hockey League. The Seattle Breakers swapped the rights to left winger Tom Martin for a used bus from the Victoria Cougars. "Actually, it was just a down payment," said Breakers owner John Hamilton. "Our old bus blew its engine on a road trip recently. Victoria had a bus they couldn't use and we had a player we couldn't use. Bingo!"

● **Someone shot** the team owner? In 1982, during the playoffs, Peter Pocklington, owner of the Edmonton Oilers, emerged from a bizarre 12-hour hostage-taking drama in his home with a bullet wound in his arm. An unemployed 29-year-old Edmonton man had held him hostage and demanded $1 million in ransom money. Police stormed the Pocklington home, firing shots that hit both Pocklington and his abductor. This happened before he traded Gretzky. After he dealt Wayne to Los Angeles, several fans threatened to shoot him.

● **In 1988,** Dino Ciccarelli of the Minnesota North Stars became the first NHL player to receive a jail term for attacking a rival player in a game. Judge Sidney Harris of Toronto sentenced Ciccarelli to one day in jail and fined him $1,000 for smashing Toronto Maple Leaf defenceman Luke Richardson over the head with his stick. While in jail, Ciccarelli signed autographs for the other prisoners.

● **Author George Tatomyr** researched the history of hockey in the Ukraine and discovered that an ill-equipped Ukrainian team named the Lions played in a Polish league in the 1930s. The Ukrainian goalie wore a primitive face mask made out of a World War I army helmet. Ukrainian hockey disappeared for several years but resurfaced in the forties. This time, the goalie wore boxing gloves and the players had to share half a dozen pair of gloves. In their debut against a German team, fans laughed at the Lions' shoddy equipment. But the Lions got the last laugh, winning 18–4.

● **In a survey of** newspaper editors and broadcasters, Team Canada's dramatic last-minute victory over the Soviet Union in 1972 was voted the greatest team accomplishment in the past 100 years. After the team fell behind in the series by 3–1–1, a nation held its breath as Paul Henderson's electrifying goal, at 19:26 of the third period in game eight in Moscow, clinched the series for Team Canada.

The survey encompassed all team sports. Hockey teams took six of the top 10 spots. The Edmonton Oilers dynasty, winners of five of seven Stanley Cups between 1983–84 and 1989–90, ranked second. The Montreal Canadiens from 1955–56 to 1959–60 were third.

● **On June 24, 1999,** Mario Lemieux, one of hockey's greatest players, was approved as the new owner of the Pittsburgh Penguins. Lemieux became the first player-turned-owner in major pro sports after he pledged $20 million to keep the franchise in Pittsburgh. Deciding to become an owner wasn't a difficult decision for the man who led the Penguins to back-to-back Stanley Cups in 1991 and '92. The team owed him $32.5 million. What better way to collect it than to own the club?

● **One of the most famous** dates in history is 9/11/01. On that date, September 11, 2001, former NHL hockey player Garnet "Ace" Bailey, director of pro scouting for the Los Angeles Kings, was late getting to Logan Airport in Boston. But he made his flight and hurried aboard United Airlines Flight 175 en route to Los Angeles. Shortly after takeoff, the flight was hijacked by terrorists and diverted to New York City, where it crashed into the south tower of the World Trade Center. All on board were killed and the tower destroyed. Bailey, 53, a member of two Stanley Cup–winning teams with Boston, in 1970 and 1972, and a scout for the Edmonton Oilers for 13 years during the eighties when the Oilers won five Stanley Cups, is remembered as a popular player and a mentor to Wayne Gretzky when he first joined the NHL.

● **Jason Spezza** has never been shy when cameras are focused on him. Did you know the Ottawa Senators star was in a baby commercial when he was 12 months old? Not long after, he was the poster boy for *Baby*, a Broadway show booked at the O'Keefe Centre in Toronto. At age five, he was featured in a commercial for Minute Maid, and two years later he was modelling kids' clothes for Kmart and Woolco. And while he once played for Don Cherry's junior team in Mississauga, it never occurred to him to dress like Grapes.

● **Did you know** that Zdeno Chara, the Boston Bruins' captain, can speak five different languages? That's a big advantage if you want to tell a referee off—and not get a penalty.

At 2 metres (6 foot 9 inches), Chara is not only the tall-
est player in hockey history, he also has the hardest shot.
He won the hardest-shot competition at the annual All-
Star Game in 2007, 2008, and 2009. His hardest was timed
at 105.9 miles per hour. Whenever he slaps me on the goal,
I feel like a rubber rocket.

● **The longest suspension** of an NHL player for his
actions on the ice occurred during the year 2000. On
February 23, Boston's Marty McSorley smashed Vancouver's
Donald Brashear across the head with his stick and was
suspended for 23 games. The sentence was later extended
to one year. The second-longest suspension was to Dale
Hunter of the Capitals, who hit the Islanders' Pierre
Turgeon into the boards after a goal on April 28, 1993.
Hunter was sidelined for 21 games.

● **On November 11, 2000,** Brad May of the Phoenix
Coyotes swung his stick, slashing Columbus Blue Jackets
forward Steve Heinze in the face, and was suspended for 20
games.

Rough body contact is part of hockey, but extreme acts
of violence should not be tolerated. If a player knew he
faced a suspension for a full season—or for life—for deliberately slugging another player with his stick, he might not
be so quick to use it as a weapon.

● **In the 1960s,** Carl Brewer was a talented defenceman
for the Toronto Maple Leafs. Clever, too. Referee Vern Buffey
often marvelled at the way Brewer could throw bigger men
off balance and make them look like awkward novices.

One night, after a brawl when gloves and sticks were
flung aside, Buffey noticed an odd-looking hockey glove

lying on the ice. The glove had no palm. Why would a player cut the palm out of his glove, Buffey wondered? When Carl Brewer claimed the glove, Buffey figured it out. In goal-mouth skirmishes, Brewer had been slipping his hands through the holes in his gloves and grabbing opponents by the sweater. He would then tug them backwards or side-ways and throw them off balance. It was a neat trick, but Buffey's discovery of Brewer's cute trick led to a new NHL rule—no more palmless hockey gloves.

⬤ **During the eighties and nineties,** Pat Verbeek was one of hockey's best right wingers. He's also a very lucky guy, because at one time it appeared his career might be over. In the spring of 1985, while working on his family's 200-acre farm near Forest, Ontario, Verbeek's left thumb was completely severed when he caught his hand in a corn plant-ing machine. The thumb dropped into a load of fertilizer, and while Pat was rushed to a hospital in nearby Sarnia, his parents searched frantically for the severed digit. One of them finally located it, packed it in ice, and drove it to the hospital, where it was reattached. But the surgeon didn't offer Verbeek much hope that the operation would be a success. "Your hockey career may be over, son," he said. "A hockey player can't grip his stick without a healthy thumb."

But soon, circulation returned to the thumb. Verbeek began lifting weights and squeezing grips to strengthen his hand. When a new season got under way, he quipped, "I think the thumb has even grown a bit because of all that fertilizer it fell in."

Verbeek made an amazing recovery. Fifteen years later, he was scoring goals at a Hall of Fame pace. In 1999–2000 as a member of the Stanley Cup–winning Dallas Stars, he joined 27 other NHLers in the 500-goal club. He finished his career with 522 goals and 1,063 points. Those look like Hall of Fame numbers to me.

● **In a 1972** game between Buffalo and Vancouver, the Canucks came up with a bold strategy. They sent five defencemen out on a power play. The Sabres responded by sending four defencemen out on the penalty kill. Wow! Nine defencemen on the ice at the same time. That had to be a hockey first.

● **In the early morning** hours of February 21, 1974, veteran defenceman Tim Horton, then with the Sabres, was racing his Italian-made sports car back to Buffalo after a game in Toronto. Police said Horton's vehicle was travelling in excess of 100 miles an hour when it left the highway and crashed. Horton was killed instantly. He was a few months away from retirement and a full-time career in the doughnut business that bore his name, a career that would have netted him riches beyond belief.

● **During the 1974–75** season, fans in Washington, DC, were able to view replays of goals and other key plays on a giant screen over centre ice at the Capital Center. Goalie John Garrett, playing for the visiting Hartford Whalers, was intrigued with the novel idea. He looked up to watch a replay and failed to see Mike Gartner of the Caps take a slapshot from long range. When the puck flew past him into the net, his coach yanked him from the game.

● **During the 1974–75** season, Don Saleski of the Philadelphia Flyers was in a horrible slump. He'd scored one goal in 31 games. During the intermission of his 32nd game, his wife agreed to take part in a fashion show at centre ice. And guess what? They booed her every step on the runway. The chap who said Philadelphia fans would boo kids who came up empty on an Easter egg hunt was right.

⬤ **What was Sadler** thinking? In 1975, he turned his back on a three-year, $250,000 contract with the Montreal Canadiens as their number one draft choice. Two years later, he tried to come back with the Edmonton Oilers. But in training camp, he said he "wasn't happy" and walked away from a two-year deal at $100,000 per year. He played in Europe for a few seasons, then retired.

⬤ **In 1977–78,** hockey's harshest penalty, a lifetime suspension, was handed to player Willie Trognitz of the IHL's Dayton Owls. Trognitz had heavily taped hands when he injured Gary McMonagle in a fight. Then he swung his stick at another player, Archie Henderson, sending him to the hospital with severe cuts to the head and a concussion.

⬤ **Marcel Bonin** played on four Stanley Cup–winning teams, once in Detroit and three times with the Montreal Canadiens. One year, hoping to change his scoring luck, he borrowed a pair of Rocket Richard's old gloves. "Maybe they'll help me get out of my slump," he told Richard. In the next eight games, Bonin scored eight goals.

Bonin is the only hockey player known to wrestle bears for a living. When he was a teenager, he made a few bucks going from town to town in Quebec following the Barnum and Bailey circus. When the ringmaster called for volunteers to wrestle a bear, Bonin was quick to enter the ring.

⬤ **What a deal!** On January 2, 1992, the Toronto Maple Leafs made a blockbuster trade with the Calgary Flames.

The Leafs acquired Doug Gilmour along with Jamie Macoun, Ric Nattress, Kent Manderville, and Rick Wamsley in return for Gary Leeman, Alex Godynyuk, Jeff Reese, Michel Petit, and Craig Berube. The 10-player deal was the largest in NHL history, and if you ask Peter Puck, one of the most lopsided.

Toronto fans loved Gilmour. He went on to have a breakout year, scoring a franchise record 127 points during the 1992–93 regular season. Gilmour was the runner-up for the Hart Trophy as regular season MVP and won the Selke Trophy as best defensive forward, the first major NHL award that a Leaf player had won since 1967.

● **Need a shorthanded goal?** Philadelphia Flyers captain Mike Richards is your man. On February 15, 2009, Richards became the first player in NHL history to score three career three-on-five shorthanded goals when he beat New York Rangers goalie Henrik Lundqvist in a 5–2 win. Six days later, on February 21, Richards became the first Flyer in team history to score a shorthanded goal in three consecutive games and the first NHL player to do so since Joe Sakic in 1998. He finished the season with a league-leading seven shorthanded goals. After his season ended, he was announced as a finalist for the Selke Trophy, along with Pavel Datsyuk of the Detroit Red Wings and Ryan Kesler of the Vancouver Canucks. Richards narrowly missed out on the Selke, which could have been Philadelphia's first individual player trophy since Eric Lindros won the Hart in 1995. Datsyuk won the vote 945–942 in the closest Selke Trophy race since its inception.

● **Hockey may be big** in Washington, DC, now, but in 1978 the franchise was in deep trouble. Owner Abe Pollin said he hoped for 10,000 season ticket holders but had sold only 4,200. The average attendance was under 10,000, down 3,899 from the previous season.

● **In 1985,** journeyman hockey player Paul Stewart, who once drew an eight-game suspension for slugging a referee and logged 1,200 penalty minutes in less than five years of pro hockey, decided he wanted to become an NHL referee. He passed all the tests and soon he was handing out penalties, not taking them.

● **Phil Kessel** of the Toronto Maple Leafs comes from an athletic family. His father, Phil Kessel Sr., was a college quarterback and was drafted by the Washington Redskins of the National Football League, spending his first year on the injured reserve list before being released. His mother, Kathy, ran track in college. Kessel has an older cousin, David Moss, who plays in the NHL, currently with the Calgary Flames. His brother, Blake, a defenceman, a draft choice of the New York Islanders, plays for the University of New Hampshire. Sister Amanda was the top scorer, with six goals and 13 assists, for the gold medal–winning Team USA at the 2009 IIHF World Women's U18 Championship.

● **On January 14, 1992,** during an Italian B Division hockey game between the Gardena and Courmayeur clubs, Miran Schrott died as the result of a stick to the chest. The stick was wielded by Italian-born Canadian Jim Boni.

Schrott, 19, and Boni, captain of the Courmayeur squad, jostled for position and Boni put his arm around Schrott's neck. Schrott punched Boni in the head. Boni reacted by bringing his stick up, hitting the defenceman in the chest with its heel. As Boni wheeled to skate away,

Schrott fell to the ice unconscious. No penalty was called. No Gardena player jumped Boni in retaliation for a perceived vicious check.

Schrott, who suffered from epilepsy, had passed out in practices before. His coach and teammates thought it nothing unusual. But this time, he never regained consciousness. The verdict was cardiac arrest.

Boni was charged with manslaughter. The Italian press crucified the transplanted Canadian. The courts were less severe. He was sentenced to one year in jail—although he didn't serve any time because he had no previous criminal record. But the incident still haunts him.

● **Two hockey Hall of Famers,** goalie Ken Dryden and forward Joe Nieuwendyk, had their college jersey numbers retired by Cornell University in 2010. There are 35 varsity athletic teams at Cornell, and the two hockey players are the only ones to have their numbers retired. As professionals, both Dryden and Nieuwendyk won two of the NHL's most coveted trophies: the Calder as rookies and the Conn Smythe as playoff MVPs. And they're the only two Cornell grads to win a Stanley Cup.

● **Ken Dryden** was drafted by the Boston Bruins in 1964, but Montreal general manager Sam Pollock quickly made a deal for him, sending two players to the Bruins, neither of whom played a single NHL game. Apparently, Dryden didn't find out about the deal until several years later. Guess he was too busy studying at Cornell. Heck, I would have told him, but I thought he knew. Besides, the Habs were so good when he played for them I didn't get close to him very often.

● **In 1994,** the New York Islanders opened the vault for their number one draft choice, Brett Lindros, signing him to a five-year, $6-million contract. Within weeks, Lindros was cut from Canada's world junior team because he didn't skate well enough. Lindros played parts of two seasons with the Islanders, scoring two goals. He was forced to retire because of concussion problems.

● **Bruce McNall** was a charming man who owned the L. A. Kings and brought Wayne Gretzky to California. When Gretzky scored his 802nd career goal on March 23, 1994, to pass Gordie Howe on the all-time goal scoring list, McNall rewarded him with a $275,000 Rolls Royce. A few months later, McNall resigned as an NHL governor and Kings president after he pleaded guilty to bank fraud, mail fraud, and conspiracy. He was accused of defrauding six banks of more than $230 million over the preceding decade. He could have been jailed for 45 years. A lenient judge sentenced him to five years and 10 months and ordered him to pay $5 million to the people he bilked.

● **In Sweden,** during the 1995–96 season, Tommie Eriksen, a 20-year-old Swedish defenceman, was handed a 90-day jail sentence after he flew into a rage in the penalty box and threw pieces of a broken stick into the crowd, injuring a young boy and a photographer. Eriksen was suspended from all sports until September 1996.

● **In his first shift** in his first game on October 20, 1995, Boston College freshman Travis Roy crashed headfirst into the boards. He had played for 11 seconds. Rushed to hospital, Roy underwent seven hours of spinal surgery, but the surgeons had bad news. He would never regain the use of his arms or legs. Today, he is in demand as a motivational speaker and he has established a foundation for spinal cord injury research. He is the only BU player to have his jersey number (24) retired.

● **A few weeks** earlier in Boston, tearful fans said farewell to the rat-infested Boston Garden and prepared to cheer the Bruins in their new multi-million dollar arena, built next door. There was a huge ovation for 47-year-old Bobby Orr, who was part of the closing ceremonies, then a much louder ovation for Normand Leveille, who skated unsteadily across the Garden ice. At age 20, Leveille's promising career as a Bruin ended when he suffered a cerebral hemorrhage during a game in Vancouver in 1982.

● **Have you ever** played in a hockey game where both teams scored more than 300 goals? If you have, you must have been one of 180 players who competed in the first annual Labatt Blue/NHL Pickup Marathon, held in Toronto from January 31 through February 3, 2000.

The event was held on the skating rink at Nathan Phillips Square. Boards were installed, as well as a time clock and benches for the two teams. Two teams of 90 players, Blues and Whites, competed in 98 periods of play stretching over 71 hours and 52 minutes. Each team comprised five squads of 15 to 18 skaters and three goaltenders. When a team grew weary, it skated off and was replaced by a fresh set of legs. The final group lasted the longest, playing for about 20 hours. Standard rules were followed, but slapshots and bodychecking were banned. The leading scorer in the unique event was Brett Punchard, a former college player at Bowling Green who racked up 37 goals and 60 points over 26 periods in the marathon. Labatt donated

$5 for every minute played to the Hockey Fights Cancer Fund—a contribution of about $10,000. And the Blues blew a 237–215 lead and lost 380–340, according to several busy statisticians.

● **From 1980 through 1984,** Warren Young's hockey career amounted to little more than a depressing bus ride through minor league cities like Nashville, Oklahoma City, Birmingham, and Baltimore. His career as a player appeared to be going nowhere. When he was invited to Pittsburgh's training camp prior to the 1984–85 season, he knew it was his last chance to make an impression. He was 28 years old, almost a doddering old man by hockey standards.

For some reason, rookie sensation Mario Lemieux, then 19, liked Young's style and asked to be placed on the same line. Despite the 10-year age difference, the two fit together like hand and glove, and Lemieux helped convert Young from an unknown minor leaguer into a big league celebrity. Young had never seen the kind of passes Mario deftly placed on his stick. He converted a large number of them into goals and finished the season with 40. He added 32 assists and won a berth on the rookie All-Star squad.

Good fortune smiled on Young again the following season, the year Detroit went on a spending spree, signing a number of free agents to million-dollar deals. Young was one of them. He signed a multi-year contract with the Wings that had him earning twice as much as Lemieux's base salary of $125,000. But without Lemieux to set him up, Young had difficulty scoring in Detroit. His goal production dropped dramatically. Even though he earned some fancy paycheques, he soon faded from the hockey scene.

⬤**Here's an account** of a game played in Montreal over a hundred years ago:

There was apparently only one topic during the day, who will win—the Wanderers or Ottawa? Tickets for the match were sold as high as twenty dollars apiece. When evening came, the crowd began to gather at the rink. The reserved seat ticket holders did not start to arrive until 8:00. But they seemed to come all at once and in a few minutes there was a jam across the front of the building, right on to St. Catherine Street. From then until after 9:00, when the game was well under way, hundreds and then thousands battled for entrance into the rink.

Holders of choice seats were held up in the rush at the front, and in some cases it took a half an hour for a party to gain admittance to the rink. Hats were broken, clothes were torn and rubbers were lost in the scrimmage. Inside and outside, the arena was damaged to an extent that beats all past records.

Inside the arena there were 80 ushers to help admit people into the arena. Policemen and ushers worked like Trojans but their efforts were small against the thousands of excited enthusiasts. Fifteen more policemen were rounded up.

Halfway through the fight for admittance, a section of the fans found the centre doors locked. They proceeded to break in the panels. They did this so effectively that not a board was left in the two big circular panels, each about two feet in diameter.

Half a dozen venturesome spirits climbed the porch and crawled over the big electric sign at the risk of losing their lives. They smashed in the windows.

Another crowd in the rear had worked their way to the roof of the annex, broke windows, but failed to gain admittance to the upper promenade. Still another group unearthed a ladder, and with this up against the wall, climbed their way to the upper promenade—again through broken windows.

Inside the rink, hundreds battled for place advantages at heads of the aisles.

When the game started they were lined up seven and eight deep. Many women were in the throng, most of them only able to catch an occasional glimpse of the play down below. The steel girders held their usual quota of daring ones. The match had started when a group of twenty-five or so rushed the gate leading up to the upper promenade, and nearly swept everything aside; policemen, ushers, doors and gates.

The excitement with which the crowd followed the game once it started was in keeping with the excitement in which they had fought their way into the building. For the full hour, there was one deafening roar from the lusty throats of thousands.

Several ladies were in a condition of collapse when they finally got into the arena. Several dresses were torn, skirts were lost and fur garments were scattered all around.

Of course, some of the players bet on the game. After the match, Pud Glass, who had played very useful hockey, was seen counting the one hundred dollars that he won.

⬤**Who invented** the curved stick? Some historians say it was Bobby Hull; others credit Stan Mikita. Former Ranger Andy Bathgate says, "I did."

Hull credits his Black Hawk teammate Stan Mikita for the invention. Mikita says, "We were at the end of a practice one day and my stick cracked in the blade. I was too tired to go fetch another stick, so I used the bent one. I took a couple of shots at the boards and the puck felt like it was moving a little faster off the blade."

After practice, Mikita and Hull took some sticks, heated the blades, and then placed them under a radiator. They applied enough force to bend the blades into a banana shape and then experimented with them on the ice. Not only did pucks fly with more velocity, but passing the puck with the banana blade resulted in quicker, more accurate passes.

Some players of that era pooh-poohed the innovation. Dave Keon and others tried the curved blades and tossed them aside. Most others jumped on the bandwagon, including amateurs.

In 1999, Hall of Famer Andy Bathgate claimed that he was the originator of the curved blade. "I used a curved blade when I was a kid playing road hockey in Winnipeg," he states. "When I turned pro with the Rangers in 1952–53, I would heat the blades of my sticks with hot water and put them under a door in the dressing room. But the problem was, the blades would straighten out in time. So Northland, my stick supplier, added fibreglass to the blades, and that kept the hook in place.

"I remember Stan Mikita grabbing a couple of my sticks from our trainer in New York. He got two goals and three assists in his next game using those sticks."

Mikita says, "Whoaaa," when told of Bathgate's claim.

"Andy's getting up there in age. I never saw Andy using a hooked stick, and I don't recall grabbing any in New York." Both men have their supporters.

● **According to an** uncredited article titled "Curved Blades Came Early" that appeared in the 1966–67 Chicago team guide, neither Hull, Mikita, nor Bathgate invented the curved blade:

> Just in case you get in an argument about who "invented" the curved stick, here's something few people know.
>
> Cy Denneny, whose Hall of Fame career spanned 1914 to 1929, says he played with a curved stick most of his career. "We didn't have any fancy machines to make our stick blades just the way we wanted them," Cy once said. "I had to stand on the blade to bend it. But let me tell you, putting a curve in the blade helps your control when you are shooting."
>
> Hall of Famer Cy Denneny should know. One year, 1920–21, he scored 34 goals in 24 games.

● **What do you think** of this deal? On March 10, 1981, the Los Angeles Kings traded a first- and a third-round draft choice for established star Rick Martin of the Buffalo Sabres. Martin had played on the famed French Connection Line in Buffalo and twice had topped 50 goals in a season. Doctors on both clubs met with Martin and assured all that he was fit to play. But when Martin arrived in L. A., he was met by the Kings' play-by-play announcer, Bob Miller, who offered him a ride to the arena. Miller became alarmed when he noticed that Martin could barely walk to his car. Martin limped through a handful of games and then retired. His knee was shot. And guess who the Sabres selected with the number one draft choice they received from the Kings? Goalie Tom Barrasso, fresh out of high school, a kid who went on to become one of the greatest netminders in the game.

● **Here's another deal** that makes me wonder what the Rangers were thinking: Following the 1975–76 season, the Rangers traded Rick "Nifty" Middleton to the Boston Bruins for veteran winger Ken Hodge. I bet I know what prompted the deal. Earlier, the Rangers had acquired Phil Esposito, Hodge's centreman when they were both with the Bruins. I'm sure Phil told management, "Get me Ken Hodge, my old winger. You'll never regret it."

Management did live to regret it.

Hodge played only one season more before his career came skidding to an end, while Middleton blossomed to become a dazzling star in Boston. He scored a hat trick in his first game as a Bruin and collected nearly 900 points in a Boston uniform over the next dozen years. He had five straight seasons of at least 40 goals and 90 points. His best season was in 1981–82, during which Middleton scored a career high 51 goals, won the Lady Byng Trophy for excellence and sportsmanship, and was named to the NHL's Second All-Star Team. The following season, he led the Bruins to the league's best regular season record and set still-unbroken records that year for the most points scored in the playoffs (33) by a player not advancing to the finals.

● **Craig Patrick** won the Sporting News Executive of the Year Award in 1998 and 1999. He is the third generation of his family to have his name engraved on the Stanley Cup and the third generation to be enshrined in the Hockey

Hall of Fame. Patrick spent two years as athletic director at the University of Denver, his alma mater, in 1988 and 1989. He was awarded the Lester Patrick Trophy, named for his grandfather, in the 1999–2000 season for his outstanding service to hockey in the United States.

Five members of the Patrick family have won the Stanley Cup, and still others have had hockey careers:

- Lester (Craig's grandfather)—Montreal Wanderers 1907 (player), Victoria Cougars 1925 (president/manager-coach), New York Rangers 1928 (playing manager-coach), 1933 (manager-coach), 1940 (manager)
- Frank (Craig's great-uncle)—Vancouver Millionaires 1915 (playing president/manager-coach)
- Lynn (Craig's father)—New York Rangers 1940 (player)
- Murray (Craig's uncle)—New York Rangers 1940 (player)
- Craig Patrick—Pittsburgh Penguins 1991, 1992 (general manager)
- Glenn (Craig's brother)—never won the Stanley Cup
- Curtiss (Craig's nephew)—minor league hockey player in the AHL and ECHL

● **Here's another story** about Wayne Gretzky, as told by Vic Symes, who was president of the Brantford Minor Hockey Association when Wayne was a pee wee player.

"I'll always remember one scene that really emphasizes Wayne's determination. He was 11 and playing in a pee wee tournament. He had 49 goals and was going for an even 50 when he took a penalty at 17:47 of the third period in the final game. Well, he sat out his penalty and stormed out of the box with 13 seconds to play. He grabbed the puck, rushed in, and scored. He reached into the net, picked up the puck, and went to the bench. I've never seen anything like that in my life. Fifty goals in one tournament, a tournament in which he played only seven games."

THIRTEEN
What More Can I Say?

Hopefully, you know a lot more about hockey now than you did before you began reading this book. But Peter Puck isn't finished yet.

The following facts are really hard to believe, but take it from me—they really are true.

⬤ **Let's go back** to a game between Boston and Chicago in 1964. Winger Dean Prentice of the Bruins raced in on the Chicago goal but was hauled down by the Hawks' Stan Mikita. Prentice crashed heavily into the boards and lay there semi-conscious. Meanwhile, the referee had awarded him a penalty shot. Even though he was still groggy, Prentice took the penalty shot—and scored! Moments later, while sitting on the Boston bench, he found he could barely move. He was rushed to hospital, where doctors diagnosed a fractured vertebrae—a broken back. Dino was laid up for a long time. Even he can't explain how he scored a penalty shot goal with a broken back.

⬤ **There's a battered puck** in the Hockey Hall of Fame in Toronto that is truly unique. It was the only puck used during a game between Minnesota and Los Angeles back in the seventies. At that time, NHL officials calculated that 20 to 30 pucks were used during the course of a normal game. Today, with more protective screening, fewer pucks are required.

● **Ever wonder** how hockey pucks are made? Huge batches of rubber mixed with carbon black—coal dust— are churned out of a machine in a roll of rubber similar to a huge sausage. The rubber sausage is sliced into 175-gram (6 ounce) pucks called blanks that are then placed in moulds, 27 blanks per mould. Team logos are glued onto the blanks, which are placed in an oven where they're "cooked" for 20 minutes and pressed under a 900-kilogram (2,000 pound) weight. The pucks are then removed, cooled, buffed, and boxed, ready for delivery.

● **Every team,** at all levels of hockey, uses hundreds of hockey pucks each season. Pucks are 7.6 centimetres (3 inches) in diameter, 2.5 centimetres (1 inch) thick, and each weighs approximately 170 grams (6 ounces).

● **NHL game pucks** have the home team's logo imprinted on them. When Don Cherry coached in Boston, he accused his bosses of being "cheap" because the pucks the Bruins purchased were simple black ones with no logos.

● **Don Cherry** went from a coaching career, first in Boston, then in Colorado, to an amazing broadcasting career with *Hockey Night in Canada*. In 1980, when his job in Colorado was in jeopardy, a newspaper poll of fans was overwhelmingly in favour of retaining Cherry—3,025 to 59. Two days later, he was fired. In leaving, he said, "It's pretty hard to fly like an eagle when you're mixed up with turkeys."

⬤ **Come on now,** how did this guy get inducted into the Hall of Fame? Old-time player Shorty Green's name is listed alphabetically on the list of Hockey Hall of Fame members, just before Wayne Gretzky's and right after Michel Goulet's. When you compare the stats of the three inductees, you can't help but wonder how Shorty made it into the Hall. And yes, Green was a forward.

Member	Games	Goals	Assists	Points	Year Inducted
Goulet	1,089	548	604	1,152	1998
Green	103	33	20	53	1962
Gretzky	1,487	894	1963	2857	1999

⬤ **Over half a century ago,** the Montreal Royals, a farm club for the Canadiens, played a road game at the Boston Garden. At first they thought the referee had failed to show up. But he was there, sitting high over the ice in a basket, like those found on a helium-filled balloon. Someone figured the official would have a better view of the action from 15 metres (50 feet) above the ice surface. The bizarre experiment lasted just one game.

⬤ **On December 12, 1933,** Toronto star Ace Bailey was almost killed in a game in Boston. A vicious check from behind by Bruins defenceman Eddie Shore sent Bailey spinning to the ice and he was rushed to hospital with a fractured skull. Bailey survived, but he never played again. Shore was suspended for 16 games. Bailey's father, toting a gun, rushed to Boston, intending to shoot Eddie Shore, but he was disarmed and sent back to Toronto. Later in the season, the league staged a benefit game for Bailey and his family. It was against

Boston, and Shore was there. When Bailey shook Shore's hand, indicating he carried no grudge, the crowd roared its approval.

● **The hockey world** was stunned when Howie Morenz, the game's greatest star, died in the spring of 1937 at age 34. Morenz was recuperating in hospital from a broken leg when his stout heart gave out. His coffin was placed at centre ice at the Montreal Forum, the scene of his greatest triumphs. The date was March 11, 1937.

There has never been a more solemn occasion in the long history of the Montreal Canadiens. The arena was jammed to capacity with his devoted fans. Morenz's flower-banked bier was passed by an endless line of teary-eyed people, young and old, who had come to pay their respects to the Mitchell, Ontario, native, a magnificent athlete. There were hundreds of floral arrangements, even floral 7s—his uniform number, a numeral that, in retirement, would never grace the back of any other Canadien. "He was the greatest of all time," lamented coach Dick Irvin. Morenz would later be named "the best player of the half-century."

Earlier in the 1936–37 season, on January 28, Montreal's 6–5 victory over Chicago had been overshadowed by an alarming incident in the first period. Morenz darted after a puck and was bodychecked by Earl Seibert of the Black Hawks. Morenz's skate blade caught in a crack in the boards and, imbedded there, his leg twisted around and snapped with a crack that could he heard throughout the arena. In an instant his season was over—and almost surely his fabulous career.

Seibert was absolved of all blame and did not receive a penalty on the play. Some people said Morenz died of a broken heart—because he knew he would never skate again.

● **For 17 years,** hardrock defenceman Larry Zeidel had bulled his way through three minor leagues, leading all of them in penalty minutes. When six new teams joined the NHL for the 1967–68 season, most of the expansion teams considered Zeidel "too old." But he came up with a novel way to sell himself to the new owners. He invested $150 and prepared a glossy resumé, extolling his virtues as a hockey player. The resumés were mailed to all six new teams. Keith Allen, general manager of the Philadelphia Flyers, read one and was impressed. At that point in his career, Zeidel had spent nearly 2,500 minutes in the penalty box, time equal to more than 40 full games. Zeidel was offered a tryout. Even though he'd been away from the NHL since 1954, he had no difficulty making the Flyers. He helped them to a first-place finish in the West Division of the NHL. After a second season with the team, he retired from the game.

● **During the 1982–83** NHL season, a snowstorm swept through New England and prevented NHL referee Ron Fournier and linesman Dan Marouelli from getting to a game in Hartford featuring the Whalers and the New York Islanders. Linesman Ron Foyt, who made it to the game on time, took over as the lone referee. But he needed two linesmen, so Foyt recruited a player from each club to wear the striped shirts. Gary Howatt of the Islanders and Mickey Vulcan of the Whalers, both of whom had minor injuries, volunteered. Both were happy to assist Foyt because "it was a once-in-a-lifetime" opportunity.

● **In 1902,** a Montreal team left by train for Ottawa and a big game with the Senators. But Montreal's star player, Charlie Liffiton, was unable to get off work in time to catch the train. The Montreal manager chartered a special train for Liffiton—at a cost of $114. After work, Liffiton hopped aboard the "special." The train and its single passenger left Montreal at 6:20 p.m. and arrived in Ottawa a few minutes ahead of game time. Was the effort worth it? Indeed it was, for Liffiton, who was averaging a goal a game, paced Montreal to a 4–2 victory.

● **In 1924,** the Toronto Granites represented Canada in hockey at the first Olympic Games, at Chamonix, France. The Granites won their first three games by 30–0, 22–0, and 33–0. Then, in what was called the roughest game ever played, Canada defeated the United States 6–1 for the Olympic gold. Canada's Harry Watson averaged more than five goals per game, scoring 36 times. It seemed that every time Watson shot me, I wound up in the net. All the pro teams wanted Watson and offered him barrels of money, but he turned them all down to enter the business world. Even though his amateur career was short, he was inducted into the Hockey Hall of Fame in 1962.

● **In Winnipeg**, a few years ago, a 48-year-old woman rivalled any pro player in the NHL for shooting accuracy. And in doing so, she won a cool $58,000 in prize money. Joan Palmer, a grandmother of four, was selected to try her shooting luck during the intermission of a Winnipeg Jets–Detroit Red Wings game at the Winnipeg Arena. Her challenge was to shoot a 7.6-centimetre (3 inch) puck through a tiny 8.25-centimetre (3 1/4 inch) opening 36 metres (120 feet) away. Palmer was allowed just one shot, and she turned it into the shot of a lifetime. The puck slid straight toward the net and slipped through the hole. Her prize was $58,000—five times her annual salary as a Pink Lady courier.

⬤ **In a similar** shootout in Oshawa, Ontario, hockey fan Dave Duncan's chances to win the $8,000 prize were nil. What's amazing is that Duncan was legally blind. Still, he cradled me on his stick and I wished him good luck. Then he sent a perfectly aimed shot three-quarters of the distance down the ice and I slid right through the hole. Boy, was I happy for Dave. It was one of the most amazing on-ice feats I've ever seen.

⬤ **I'll bet you** can't name the oldest rookie to play in the NHL. When the NHL expanded from six to 12 teams in 1967–68, the St. Louis Blues plucked defenceman Connie Madigan from the minor leagues. Madigan was 38 years old when he got his first big league chance.

Madigan played 20 regular season games and five play-off games, collecting three assists, and then was released. He later played a bit part as Ross "Mad Dog" Madison in the classic hockey movie *Slap Shot*.

⬤ **Strange numbers** have appeared on the backs of hockey jerseys. A junior goalie named Gunn wore number 45 on his back as a pun on his name and on the famous .45 calibre revolver. A player in England wore number 102.1 one season to advertise the FM radio station he worked for. And goalie Bernie Parent, when he played with the Philadelphia Blazers of the WHA, wore 00 on his jersey. Whenever the puck crossed his goal line, I'd hear Bernie say, "Oh, oh."

● **On June 18, 1987,** New York Rangers general manager Phil Esposito traded a number one draft choice and $75,000 to the Quebec Nordiques—not for a player but a coach! Esposito paid a high price to bring Nords coach Michel Bergeron to Broadway. Their relationship, however, soon cooled. After working together for a few months, Espo fired Bergeron.

● **You've seen coaches** call a time out late in a game and huddle with their players at the bench. When he coached the Colorado Rockies, Don Cherry called a time out during a big game against the Boston Bruins, his former team. But he delivered no pep talk. To the delight of the fans, Cherry turned his back on his players and signed autographs for people in the crowd. You can bet his bosses back in Colorado weren't thrilled to see him do that. But the Rockies won the game, so what could they say?

● **The CBC conducted** a poll a few years ago, asking viewers to name the top 10 Canadians of all time. Don Cherry finished seventh. He's the only one on the list who hasn't received an Order of Canada.

● **Ray Scapinello** was a linesman in the NHL for 33 years. He officiated in more than 2,500 regular season and 426 playoff games—and never missed an assignment! He's a worthy member of the Hockey Hall of Fame, inducted in 2008.

● **Igor Larionov** didn't arrive in the NHL until he was 29 years old. The Russian star played two seasons with the Vancouver Canucks, two seasons with the San Jose Sharks, and another eight seasons with the Detroit Red Wings, where he won three Stanley Cups. Better late than never was Igor's motto.

● **Sergei Makarov,** who was two years older than Larionov, became the oldest player to win the Calder Trophy as NHL rookie of the year. Makarov was 31 in 1989–90. Before joining the Calgary Flames, Makarov had played professionally in the Soviet Union for a dozen years. After Makarov's win, the NHL declared that all future Calder Trophy winners must be 26 years of age or younger by September 15 of their rookie season.

And a good thing, too. The Calder should go to a young guy, not some old fellow who's approaching retirement.

● **The Calder Trophy** is one of the few major individual awards Wayne Gretzky didn't win. In 1979–80, even though he tallied 137 points in his first NHL season, a first-year record, Gretzky was ruled ineligible for the rookie award because he had played the previous season in the World Hockey Association. Peter Stastny, a veteran of European hockey, won the Calder in 1980 with 109 points. A lot of fans didn't think it was fair. Peter Puck didn't think so, either.

● **I must admit** Peter Stastny enjoyed a fabulous NHL career with 450 career goals and a Hall of Fame berth. His brothers also became hockey stars. After Peter and his brother Anton defected from Czechoslovakia to join the Quebec Nordiques, their older brother Marian soon joined them. Only twice before had three brothers played on the same team in the NHL—the Bentley brothers in Chicago and the Plager brothers in St. Louis. Now Peter has two sons in the league, Jan and Paul.

● **Here's something interesting.** Roger Barnsley, a Canadian psychologist, gathered statistics on hundreds of junior A hockey players and found that more players were born in January than in any other month. His study revealed that 40 per cent of the top players were born between January and March, 30 per cent between April and June, 20 per cent between July and September, and only 10 per cent between October and December. In his book *The Outliers*, author Malcolm Gladwell gives a simple explanation. The cutoff for age-class hockey is January 1. Kids born in January are more mature than kids born many months later. Bigger and stronger, they are selected by coaches for all-star teams and travel teams. They are likely to get better coaching and more ice time than younger teammates.

● **Marty St. Louis** is small—like me. He says he's 5 foot 9, but that must be with his skates on. St. Louis was a fabulous scorer in college hockey at the University of Vermont. In four seasons there, after becoming an All-American and two-time nominee for the Hobey Baker award as MVP, and after finishing his college career four points shy of the Eastern College Athletic Conference all-time scoring record, he was ignored by all the NHL teams. Not one of them drafted him. Eventually he signed a free agent contract with the Calgary Flames, who gave up on him. He then signed with Tampa Bay and quickly rose to stardom. In 2003–04, St. Louis won the Hart Trophy (MVP), the Art Ross Trophy (scoring leader), the Pearson Trophy (now the Ted Lindsay Trophy, players' choice as MVP), and the Stanley Cup. Not bad for a little fellow from Laval, Quebec, who ignored the people who judged him "too small for the NHL."

● **In 1916,** a team of amateur players from Sudbury, Ontario, was invited to play a weekend series of games in Cleveland and Pittsburgh against two professional clubs. The Northern Ontario boys eagerly accepted, although they were at a disadvantage. They'd never played on artificial ice before, and they'd never seen a rink as big as Pittsburgh's—100 feet wide and 300 feet long. Wearing woolen jerseys and socks, they sweated buckets in the heated arenas. They lost three of four games, but it was an enjoyable adventure—until they returned home. Then they were slapped with a season-long suspension for agreeing to play professionals. No official or group had warned them not to go on the junket. They were confused and furious. Hockey had some tough rules in those days.

● **Noel Picard** of the St. Louis Blues became rattled one night during a game against Boston. During a line change, he skated to the wrong bench. This is unheard of in hockey. The Boston trainer opened the gate for Picard and the big guy sat down among all the Bruins. Then he looked around and was shocked to find himself sitting with the opposing team. By then, the play had begun. But Picard was too embarrassed to sit there. He leaped over the boards and made a beeline for the St. Louis bench. The referee caught him and gave the Blues a two-minute penalty for too many men on the ice. Scotty Bowman, the Blues' coach, was irate. And who could blame him?

● **When he played** for the St. Louis Blues, winger George Morrison sat on the bench game after game. In Los Angeles one night, an usher whispered to him, "George, can I have your stick after the game?" Bored and hungry, Morrison replied, "Sneak me a hot dog and a coke and you can have my stick." Moments later, the usher slipped Morrison the hot dog and the drink. That's when coach Bowman roared, "Morrison, get out there and kill that penalty!"

Caught by surprise, Morrison knocked the drink off the bench and quickly stuffed the hot dog down the cuff of his hockey glove. But when he leaped on the ice, an opposing player slammed into him and the hot dog flew in the air, mustard and relish sailing in all directions.

Only when he retired did Morrison confess he once carried a hot dog into an NHL game.

● **Wayne Cashman** played left wing on one of Boston's most prolific lines with Phil Esposito at centre and Ken Hodge on right wing. Espo counted on Cashman to do the dirty work in the corners and to get the puck into the slot by fair means or foul. And if someone gave Orr or Espo a cheap shot, Cashman would be there in an instant, exacting revenge. When veterans Serge Savard of the Winnipeg Jets and Carol Vadnais of the New Jersey Devils retired from hockey a few days before Cashman's last game in 1983, it made the Bruins left winger, at 38, the oldest survivor of the Original Six league.

Off the ice, Cashman was a master of mischief. Once he broke his foot while swinging on a chandelier, and in Los Angeles one night, when the anthem singer was about to perform before a crucial playoff game, Cashman spoiled the soloist's rendition by impishly cutting the microphone cord with his skate. In 1970, after the Bruins won the Stanley Cup, he played traffic cop during the celebrations that followed. He stood on a Boston intersection waving cars in all directions until there was a mammoth snarl. Reluctantly, the cops arrested him and brought him to the station, where he was told he could make one phone call. Did he phone his lawyer? Coach Don Cherry? No, his call was to a restaurant—for an order of Chinese food.

In Vancouver, on the night of November 7, 1975, when Cashman discovered the Bruins had traded his pal Phil Esposito, along with Carol Vadnais, to the hated New York Rangers, he organized a going away party for his former mates. Before it was over, there were damages of $2,000 to pay.

The following season, Cashman became team captain and the hi-jinks became less frequent.

● **On March 16, 2004,** Kings coach Andy Murray needed one more victory to become the team's winningest coach in history. Before a game with the Blues, Bob Miller, the Kings' play-by-play announcer, congratulated Murray on his accomplishment. Miller was almost certain the Kings would beat the Blues that night. But they lost that game and the one that followed. They lost again and again—11 straight times. The season ended, and Murray never did set the record.

It was how they lost that final game that almost put Murray in an asylum. The Kings were leading San Jose 3–1 with just over 20 seconds to play. Home and dried out, right? Wrong. The Sharks pulled their goalie and Brad Stuart scored to make it 3–2. A few seconds later, Stuart scored again to tie the score. You guessed it. The Sharks scored in overtime and the Kings went down for the 11th straight time.

Everybody blamed Miller. "You jinxed the coach, Bob," they said. "You congratulated him prematurely."

● **If Bobby Orr** was the best defenceman ever to wear Boston colours, then Eddie Shore was second best.

Shore was an NHL superstar defenceman who played

from 1926 to 1940—a four-time winner of the Hart Trophy and a guy who often made a grand entrance to the game, wearing a long gold dressing gown over his uniform while the band played "Hail to the Chief."

One day, Shore missed the train taking the Bruins to Montreal. So he borrowed a friend's limo—and his pal's chauffeur—and set off for Montreal through the snow-covered mountains of New Hampshire and Vermont. When the limo driver tired, Shore took the wheel himself and drove all night through a blizzard. When the limo skidded off the road into a ditch, a farmer with a team of horses hauled it out. Shore drove on, hour after hour, arriving at the Montreal Forum just before game time. Even though he was totally exhausted, he played a full 60 minutes against the Montreal Maroons that night. What's more, he slapped in the only goal of the game, making his long night's journey through the sleet and snow well worth it.

● **Dozens of NHL stars** have seen their team jerseys lifted to the arena rafters—their numbers retired forever.

But only one number—Wayne Gretzky's 99—has been retired by the entire league, assuring that no player will ever wear it again. At the 2000 All-Star Game in Toronto, in an on-ice ceremony, Gretzky and members of his family were on hand for the formal retirement ceremonies.

Gretzky wasn't the first to wear number 99. Five different players have worn it in league history. The first number 99s were Leo Bourgault and Joe Lamb, who briefly wore the double nines on their jerseys—in 1934–35 with the Montreal Canadiens.

Forty-four years later, in 1979, Gretzky arrived in the NHL wearing the 99 he'd been given in 1977 during his junior hockey days in Sault Ste. Marie.

Forward Wilf Paiement began wearing 99 after he was traded from Colorado to Toronto in December 1979.

Only a trivia expert would know the name of the fifth player to wear number 99. Rick Dudley, when he was traded from the Buffalo Sabres to the Winnipeg Jets in 1981, asked for jersey number 9. Someone told him, "That number's taken. Wear 99 instead." After a few days, the Jets played in Edmonton. When the Oiler fans saw Dudley wearing Gretzky's number, they went ballistic. Dudley was the target of their verbal abuse every time he stepped on the ice. "Oh, they gave me an awful time," he recalls. "I couldn't wait to switch to another number."

● **George Armstrong** played 20 seasons for the Toronto Maple Leafs and was team captain for more than 10 of them. Throughout his career, he was associated with champions. He played on a Memorial Cup winner, an Allan Cup winner, a Calder Cup winner (in Pittsburgh), and four Stanley Cup–winning teams.

Armstrong combined great leadership with a captivating sense of humour. Johnny Bower, his roommate on road trips, was often the victim of an Armstrong prank. In the Leaf dressing room, Bower habitually placed his dentures in a small plastic cup before skating out for a game or practice. One day, he returned to the room and popped in his teeth. But they failed to click into place. Frustrated, he pulled them out and examined them. That's when he realized they weren't his teeth. Somebody had substituted another set of dentures during his absence. He looked across the room at Armstrong, who was trying to hold back his laughter. "Damn you, Chief," fumed Bower. "You did this. Where'd you get these dentures—from a dentist?" "No way," laughed Armstrong. "I got them from an undertaker."

It was Armstrong who scored the goal that wrapped up the last Toronto Stanley Cup triumph, in 1967. With the Leafs leading the Canadiens three games to two (Montreal rode the crest of a 15-game undefeated streak into the finals) and nursing a 2–1 lead into the final minute of play in game six, Armstrong scored into an empty net with 47 seconds left on the clock to assure a Toronto victory and the team's 11th Stanley Cup.

● **During a 1981** playoff battle between the Quebec Nordiques and the Philadelphia Flyers, Nordiques goaltender Dan Bouchard, a born-again Christian who believed in the Golden Rule, found himself in a wrestling match with diminutive but scrappy Ken Linesman of the Flyers.

Linesman had no compunction about breaking a few rules, written or otherwise. When Bouchard tried to disengage himself from Linesman's grasp, he felt a sharp pain. "The so-and-so bit me on the hand," Bouchard said angrily. "Now I know why everyone calls him Rat."

● **The Detroit Red Wings** once had a player named Fern Gauthier who scored so infrequently that his teammates kept ribbing him. "Fern, you can't put the puck in the ocean," they kidded.

One day in New York City, Fern took a few pucks and a stick down to the docks on Manhattan Island. Gordie Howe tagged along as a witness. Gauthier soon proved, once and for all, that he could indeed put a puck in the ocean. But not without difficulty. Howe claimed he missed on his first two shots—on one, a seagull swooped down and grabbed the puck in midair; on the second, his shot landed on a passing barge. But his third shot hit a wave and sank from sight.

Gauthier threw both arms in the air to celebrate. Howe applauded, the gulls squawked, and Gauthier called it his proudest moment in hockey.

A Final Word

That's it, hockey fans.

I hope you enjoyed reading *Peter Puck's Big Book of Hockey*. Now for some final words of advice from your poke check professor.

⬤ **When you play** the game, play to win, but always play for fun.

⬤ **Respect your opponents** on the ice and always play fair.

⬤ **Respect the referees** and linesmen. They may not make all the right calls, but they're doing their best. Officiating is not an easy job.

⬤ **Listen to your coaches.** They have years of experience, and hopefully they can help teach you a few little tricks and tactics that will improve your game.

⬤ **Make sure you wear** skates that fit snugly, and use a stick that's neither too long nor too short.

⬤ **Remember it's a team game.** It's fun to score goals, but assists are important, too.

● **Focus on the three** S's of hockey: skating, stickhandling, and shooting.

● **And for all of you** involved in minor hockey, don't forget to thank your folks and other people in your life who drive you to games and practices, who encourage you to do your best, who talk to you about being modest when you win and gracious when you lose.

Have fun on the ice.
Your friend in hockey,
Peter Puck